HOTSPOTS
CYPRUS

Written by George McDonald, updated by Carole French
Front cover photography courtesy of Thomas Cook Tour Operations Ltd

Original concept by Studio 183 Limited
Series design by Bridgewater Books
Cover design/artwork by Lee Biggadike, Studio 183 Limited

Produced by the Bridgewater Book Company
The Old Candlemakers, West Street, Lewes, East Sussex BN7 2NZ, United Kingdom
www.bridgewaterbooks.co.uk
Project Editor: Emily Casey Bailey
Project Designer: Lisa McCormick

Published by Thomas Cook Publishing
A division of Thomas Cook Tour Operations Limited
PO Box 227, Units 15-16, Coningsby Road, Peterborough PE3 8SB, United Kingdom
email: books@thomascook.com
www.thomascookpublishing.com
+ 44 (0) 1733 416477

ISBN-13: 978-1-84157-523-0
ISBN-10: 1-84157-523-2

First edition © 2006 Thomas Cook Publishing
Text © 2006 Thomas Cook Publishing
Maps © 2006 Thomas Cook Publishing
Head of Thomas Cook Publishing: Chris Young
Project Editor: Diane Ashmore
Production/DTP Editor: Steven Collins

Printed and bound in Spain by Graficas Cems, Navarra, Spain

All rights reserved. No part of this publication may be reproduced, stored in a retrieval system or transmitted, in any form or by any means, electronic, mechanical, recording or otherwise, in any part of the world, without prior permission of the publisher. Requests for permission should be made to the publisher at the above address.

Although every care has been taken in compiling this publication, and the contents are believed to be correct at the time of printing, Thomas Cook Tour Operations Limited cannot accept any responsibility for errors or omission, however caused, or for changes in details given in the guidebook, or for the consequences of any reliance on the information provided. Descriptions and assessments are based on the author's views and experiences when writing and do not necessarily represent those of Thomas Cook Tour Operations Limited.

CONTENTS

SYMBOLS KEY 4	Pissouri & Kouklia........................80
INTRODUCTION........................5	The Troodos Mountains 82
Map of Cyprus 6	Troodos wine villages................88
Getting to know Cyprus 8	Cruising to Egypt & the Greek Islands.....................92
The best of Cyprus 10	
RESORTS 13	**LIFESTYLE** 95
Lefkosia (Nicosia)..............14	Food and drink 96
Agia Napa (Ayia Napa) 27	Menu decoder 100
Protaras..............32	Shopping 102
Larnaka (Larnaca) 36	Kids 104
Lemesos (Limassol)..............42	Sports & activities 106
Pafos (Paphos) 50	Festivals & events 108
Coral Bay & Pegeia 58	**PRACTICAL INFORMATION** 111
Polis & Latsi (Latchi)..............62	Preparing to go..............112
EXCURSIONS 65	During your stay..............117
Stavrovouni & Lefkara 66	**INDEX** 125
Cape Kiti & Amathous 70	**ACKNOWLEDGEMENTS**........128
The Akrotiri Peninsula 74	
Kourion & the Sanctuary of Apollo Ylatis 78	

HOTSPOTS

SYMBOLS KEY

The following is a key to the symbols used throughout this book:

i information office	police station	restaurant
bus station	airport	café
post office	tip	bar
church	shopping	fine dining

- telephone
- fax
- email
- website address
- address
- opening times
- important

€ budget price €€ mid-range price €€€ most expensive

★ specialist interest ★★ see if passing ★★★ top attraction

INTRODUCTION
Getting to know Cyprus

INTRODUCTION

Getting to know Cyprus

Cyprus is a Mediterranean holiday island par excellence that extends a warm welcome to visitors and has much to offer. Sunshine, blue skies, beaches, vineyards, orange and lemon groves, a multicoloured carpet of flowers in spring, wild mountain ranges, cedar forests and remote villages are all to be discovered on this beautiful island.

APHRODITE'S ISLAND
In Greek mythology, Aphrodite, the goddess of love, was born here, drifting ashore on a seashell. As the Homeric Hymn to Aphrodite tells it:
> *I will sing of stately Aphrodite, gold-crowned and beautiful,*
> *Whose dominion is the walled cities of all sea-set Cyprus.*
> *There the moist breath of the West Wind wafted her over the*
> *waves of the loud-moaning sea.*

Cypriots have taken Aphrodite to their hearts, and who can blame them?

HISTORY
Stone Age tombs, Greek temples, Roman mosaics, Byzantine monasteries, Crusader castles, Gothic abbeys, Arab mosques, Turkish bath-houses, Imperial British hill stations – where else but Cyprus? The island has always been a crossroads and visiting civilizations left the signature of their passing in many ruined historic sites.

CLIMATE
With around 3000 hours of sunshine annually, Cyprus is well acquainted with that golden ball in the sky. From spring through to autumn, good weather is pretty well guaranteed, with summer temperatures soaring into the 30s°C (90s°F). Spring and autumn are milder, with the possibility of rain. Even in winter, the climate can be warm, although mixed with periods of rain, and even snow in the Troodos Mountains. If you find yourself caught in a rainstorm, you can take comfort from the fact that the island badly needs the water to restore reservoirs and underground supplies that have been depleted by drought.

INTRODUCTION

BEACHES

Cyprus has good if not very extensive beaches around Agia Napa, Protaras, Larnaka, Lemesos and Pafos, and at points in between. There are also tiny beaches in the rugged Akamas Peninsula, and some very quiet ones along the north coast east of Polis. Most of the popular beaches have a range of services that may include lounger and umbrella hire, beach cafés and restaurants, pedalos, and water sports facilities.

Remember to take safety seriously on the beach and in the sea, especially with young children – calm as the seas around Cyprus look, they are subject to very strong currents. And be careful not to overdo the sunbathing, particularly at the beginning of your holiday, and once again particularly with children.

GEOGRAPHY

Lefkosia is the capital, and lies in the middle of the island, at the heart of the agricultural Mesaoria Plain. Just as Cyprus is a divided island at present, Lefkosia is a divided capital. The Cyprus army is on one side of the Green Line, facing Turkish occupation troops on the other side, with United Nations peacekeepers in the middle. Notable places in the Turkish-occupied area are the Pentadaktylos Mountains, the resort of Kerynia (Kyrenia) and the once opulent medieval city of Ammochostos (Famagusta).

The south-coast resorts around Agia Napa and Protaras offer an escape that many sun-starved north Europeans dream of, while Larnaka and Lemesos act as both important business centres and holiday resorts. In the west, Pafos is another important resort area. North of Pafos, the small resorts of Polis and Latsi lie between the Akamas Peninsula wilderness to the west and the relatively untouched north-east coast.

A little way inland from the coast, you enter a different Cyprus, a place of timeless villages and rugged scenery, reaching up to the windy heights of the Troodos Mountains, and the 1952 m (nearly 6500 ft) summit of Mount Olympus. There are Byzantine monasteries and churches, tranquil villages and hard-working farmers who produce a cornucopia of fruits, vegetables and grapes for wine.

INTRODUCTION

The best of Cyprus

Cyprus has a wide range of fascinating places to see and visit. Many of them are either archaeological or religious in nature, reflecting the island's long and colourful history.

Baths of Aphrodite (page 105)
According to legend, this pool of fresh water at the beginning of the Akamas Peninsula is where Aphrodite, the Greek goddess of love, bathed.

Choirokoitia Neolithic Village (page 71)
The foundations of circular homes occupy a bleak hillside near Larnaka. They were occupied from the 7th to the 4th century BC by Stone Age people who buried their dead under the floors.

Cyprus Archaeological Museum (page 16)
Lefkosia's top museum houses a superb historical collection, including the Aphrodite of Soli and a bronze statue of Roman Emperor Septimius Severus.

Green Line (page 19)
This grim reminder of Cyprus's divided status runs through Lefkosia from east to west. The Ledra Palace Hotel checkpoint is the main crossing point for visitors from the south to the north of Lefkosia.

Hala Sultan Tekke (pages 38 and 72)
This notable mosque stands on the shore of Larnaka's Salt Lake, and incorporates the tomb of the Hala Sultan, a relative of the Prophet Mohammed, who died in Cyprus in AD 649.

Kolossi Castle (page 75)
This castle near Lemesos was the Grand Commandery of the Knights of the Order of St John of Jerusalem, later of the Knights Templar, after the Crusaders were driven out of the Holy Land in 1291.

🔺 *Tombs of the Kings, Pafos*

Kourion (page 78)

Visit the ruins of an ancient city, on a clifftop overlooking the sea, west of Lemesos.

Lara Bay (page 60)

On the western shore of Akamas Peninsula, this is the home of the Lara Turtle Project, which protects endangered green and loggerhead turtles.

Larnaka Fort (page 38)

Larnaka Fort was built in 1625, and occupies a dramatic position overlooking the sea.

Lefkara (page 67)

In this village in the Troodos foothills, women sit outdoors in good weather threading handmade lace in the traditional style, called *lefkaritika*.

Mount Olympus (page 85)

The highest peak of the Troodos range, Mount Olympus reaches almost 1952 m (nearly 6500 ft). In winter you can ski.

INTRODUCTION

Omodos (page 90)
This is a restored village that lies in the foothills of the Troodos Mountains, where several arts and crafts workshops have been established and residents invite visitors for guided tours of their traditional homes.

Pafos Mosaics (page 53)
A cluster of buildings from the Roman period that house superb mosaics showing scenes from Greek mythology.

Rock of Aphrodite (page 80)
An unusual rock formation in the sea beside the Lemesos–Pafos road. This is the legendary spot where Aphrodite, the Greek goddess of love was born and was washed ashore on a seashell.

Sanctuary of Aphrodite (page 80)
This shrine to the Greek goddess of love at the village of Kouklia was renowned throughout the ancient Mediterranean.

Sanctuary of Apollo Ylatis (page 79)
This was an important temple and place of pilgrimage in ancient times, located west of Kourion. Dormitories and halls can be clearly seen, along with the Priest of Apollo's house and the partially restored Temple of Apollo.

Stravrovouni Monastery (page 66)
Stavrovouni perches on top of a 610 m (2000 ft) rocky outcrop with a view over the desolate landscape between Lefkosia and Larnaka. St Helena founded the monastery in AD 327.

Tombs of the Kings (page 55)
Dating from the 3rd century BC to the 3rd century AD, this is a complex of rock-cut tombs beside the sea, in which leading citizens of Pafos were buried.

RESORTS
Places under the sun

RESORTS

Lefkosia (Nicosia)
churches and minarets

The city of Lefkosia (Nicosia) is a modern and sophisticated capital. At its heart is Old Lefkosia, scarred by the 'Green Line' that separates the south from the Turkish-controlled north. Political events relating to the Cyprus problem and the EU accession have resulted in the partial opening of checkpoints to Cypriots as well as to tourists from abroad who choose to make the day's visit to the other side.

At the same time, the inner city is, in places, a glorious evocation of times past, with its crumbling – and now increasingly restored – mud-brick and sandstone houses. These are jumbled in with mosques from whose minarets the faithful are summoned to prayer, Orthodox churches glimmering with lamps and icons, and Ottoman baths, inns and villas.

 Lefkosia's tourist information office is at 11 Aristokyprou Street, Laiki Geitonia ❶ 22 67 42 64

◯ *The statue of Makarios at the Archbishop's Palace*

LEFKOSIA

> **GUIDED TOURS**
> Walking tours are offered free of charge by the Lefkosia
> Municipality. They include: Walking Tour of Lefkosia (Thursdays);
> Chrysaliniotissa and Kaimakli – The Past Restored (Mondays);
> Lefkosia – Outside the Walls (Fridays). Tours in English depart at
> 10.00 hours from the Cyprus Tourist Organisation office in the
> old town. ⓐ 11 Aristokyprou Street, Laiki Gitonia ⓘ 22 67 42 64

THINGS TO SEE & DO
Agia Faneromeni ★
Holds the tombs of Archbishop Kyprianos and several Orthodox bishops who were among 500 leading Greek Cypriots executed by the Ottoman authorities in 1821 during the revolt of mainland Greece against Turkish rule. The tiny Arablar Mosque beside the church is worth visiting.
ⓐ Onasagorou Street ⓑ Open irregularly ⓘ Admission free

Agios Ioannis Cathedral ★★
Lefkosia's splendid little Orthodox cathedral stands beside the Archbishop's Palace. Built in 1662, it has an abundance of murals and icons, with gilt decoration and sparkling coloured lamps. The pulpit is graced with a magnificent double-headed eagle, the emblem of Byzantium ⓐ Archiepiskopou Kyprianou Plateia (within the Archbishopric) ⓑ Open Mon–Fri 08.00–noon and 14.00–16.00, Sat 08.00–noon (and during Mass) ⓘ Admission free

Archbishop's Palace ★
The resplendent palace of the Archbishop of Cyprus dates from 1960 and includes the modest private apartments of its first occupant, Archbishop Makarios, late Ethnarch of the Cypriot Orthodox Church and first President of the Republic of Cyprus. A gigantic statue of Makarios stands in the grounds. ⓐ Archiepiskopou Kyprianou Plateia (within the Archbishopric) ⓑ Occasionally open to the public for organized visits

RESORTS

Athalassa Forest Park ★★
This park is a wide expanse of forest and fresh air on the city's doorstep. There are Forestry Service nurseries here, and a small lake with waterbirds and picnic areas. It makes a pleasant change of pace and scenery for anyone who has had too much of the busy traffic and broiling heat of Lefkosia in summer. ⓐ Off Leoforos Lemesos near the start of the motorway to Larnaka ⓘ Visitor Centre: 22 46 29 43 ⓒ Open permanently ⓘ Admission free

Bayraktar Mosque ★
This mosque is also called the Standard Bearer's Mosque because it supposedly occupies the place where the first Turkish standard bearer to plant the Ottoman banner on the walls during the final assault of the 1570 siege was killed. He was buried in this mosque, which was built in his honour. The mosque stands beside a city bus station and is surrounded by gardens. ⓐ Constanza Bastion (off Leoforos Konstantinou Palaiologou) ⓒ Generally closed to visitors

Byzantine Museum and Art Galleries ★
This museum displays an impressive Orthodox icon collection. Photography is forbidden here and you must leave your camera at the ticket office. ⓐ Archiepiskopou Kyprianou Plateia (within the Archbishopric) ⓘ 22 43 00 08 ⓒ Open Mon–Fri 09.00–16.30, Sat 09.00–13.00, closed Sun ⓘ Admission charge

Cyprus Archaeological Museum ★★★
The museum takes you on a journey through time, by way of a superb collection of historical finds, beginning in the Stone Age around 7000 BC and ending at the downfall of the Roman Empire. The objects on display include 2000 Bronze Age terracotta figurines found at the Sanctuary of Agia Eirini. There is also the superb Aphrodite of Soli and a larger-than-life bronze statue of the Roman Emperor Septimius Severus. ⓐ Mouseiou Street ⓘ 22 86 58 64 ⓒ Open Mon–Sat 09.00–17.00, Sun 10.00–13.00 ⓘ Admission charge

RESORTS

 Good spots for a shady picnic can be found among the trees of the Municipal Gardens opposite the Cyprus Archaeological Museum on Leoforos Mouseiou.

Eleftheria Plateia ★
Lefkosia's main square occupies a bridge over the dried-up moat around the Venetian walls and is a popular meeting place. ⓐ Adjacent to Ledra Street, the main shopping thoroughfare in Lefkosia

Ethnographical Museum ★★
Take a glimpse at the lifestyles of ordinary people in Cyprus during the 19th and early 20th centuries by visiting this collection of costumes, tapestry, embroidery, pottery and wood carvings. ⓐ Archiepiskopou Kyprianou Plateia (within the Archbishopric) ⓣ 22 43 25 78 ⓛ Open Mon–Fri 09.00–13.30, closed Sat and Sun ⓘ Admission charge

Famagusta Gate ★
One of three original fortified gateways in the Venetian walls, this one had fallen into disrepair before being restored and given a new lease of life as the city's Municipal Cultural Centre. You can visit temporary art exhibitions, experimental theatre and other cultural events in its stone-built galleries, and bar hop at trendy cafés in the area. ⓐ Pyli Ammochostou (off Leoforos Athinas) ⓣ 22 43 08 77 ⓛ Open Mon– Fri 10.00–13.00 and 17.00–20.00 (summer); Mon–Fri 10.00–13.00 and 16.00–19.00 (winter), closed Sat and Sun ⓘ Admission free

Freedom Monument ★
This is a memorial to the struggle of the EOKA freedom fighters during the 1950s against British rule. It brought Cyprus to independence in 1960, although it did not bring the union with Greece for which EOKA had fought. Bronze statues representing priests and Cypriot civilians emerge from a marble prison as armed EOKA freedom fighters raise the bars. ⓐ Podocataro Bastion of the Venetian Walls (off Leoforos Nikiforou Foka)

LEFKOSIA

THE GREEN LINE
Almost everyone wants to see this grim reminder of the divided state of Cyprus, which cuts like a wound through the heart of the Old City of Lefkosia. The Green Line – so called because that was the colour of the pen used by United Nation peacekeepers to define the border on the map – runs through the city from east to west, a line of concrete-and-oil-drum barricades, ruined houses, sentry posts and fortified positions.

If you try to approach too close, you'll be stopped by the Cyprus National Guard before you get to the UN peacekeepers' positions in the middle of the two sides. Visitors can cross from the south to the north sides of Lefkosia, and vice versa, at the **Ledra Palace Hotel** checkpoint.

House of the Dragoman ★★
This splendid museum is housed in the restored 18th-century home of the Dragoman Hadjigeorgakis Kornesios, who met an untimely end in Istanbul in 1804. On the upper floor are rooms decorated in a style fit for a wealthy Ottoman official, including a divan-lined room. Downstairs are servants' quarters and storage rooms. Carved woodwork and colonnades add to the mansion's graceful lines. ❸ Patriarchou Grigoriou Street ❶ 22 30 53 16 ❷ Open Mon–Fri 08.30–15.30, closed Sat and Sun ❶ Admission charge

Ledra Palace Hotel ★
You can't stay at what was once Lefkosia's most elegant hotel, and, now a base of the UN peacekeeping force in Cyprus. You can see where it stands, though, inside the United Nations buffer zone, if you take the opportunity – not encouraged by the Greek Cypriot authorities – to pass through Lefkosia's version of Berlin's former 'Checkpoint Charlie' and visit the Turkish zone of the city. ❸ Leoforos Markou Drakou (near Pafos Gate)

RESORTS

🔺 *Orange seller at the fruit and vegetable market*

Leventis Municipal Museum ★
Situated within the renovated Laïki Geitonia district, the museum presents an interesting evocation of Lefkosia in times past.
ⓐ Ippokratous Street, Laïki Geitonia ⓣ 22 66 14 75 ⓞ Open Tues–Sun 10.00–16.30, closed Mon ⓘ Admission free

Municipal Gardens ★★
A cool place on a hot day, the park is shaded by trees and filled with flowers. You can sit on benches and stroll around on pathways, and visit fish ponds and an aviary. Its open-air Garden Café is one of the oldest and most popular cafés in Lefkosia. ⓐ Off Leoforos Mouseiou (near Pafos Gate) ⓞ Open daily ⓘ Admission free

National Struggle Museum ★
Covers the Greek Cypriot movement for freedom from British colonial rule during the 1950s, led by the EOKA guerrilla organization.

Exhibits include weaponry, photographs, clandestine materials and a mock-up of an execution cell in which convicted EOKA killers were hanged by the authorities. ⓔ 7 Plateia Arch, Kyprianou ⓘ 22 30 58 78 ⓐ Open Mon–Fri 08.00–14.00 (also Thurs 15.00–17.30, except in July and August) ⓘ Admission charge

Omeriye Mosque ★
A superb view of Lefkosia can be had from the minaret of this mosque, which, until the Ottoman conquest, had been a Catholic church. Minus shoes, you can visit the interior. ⓔ Trikoupi Street, Tillirias Plateia ⓐ Open daily ⓘ Admission free (but a donation is welcome)

Pafos Gate ★
One of three historic gateways in the Venetian walls, Pafos Gate is overlooked by Turkish flags because the Green Line runs beside it. The gate is still an important traffic artery, connecting the Old City with the new. ⓔ Pyli Pafou (at the north end of Leoforos Mouseiou)

Panagia Chrysaliniotissa ★
Our Lady of the Golden Flax is one of the most beautiful old churches in Lefkosia, dating from the 15th century. Its dusky interior is embellished with icons and gilt ornamentation. ⓔ Odysseos Street ⓐ Open irregularly ⓘ Admission free

Race Course ★★
Take a break from cultural tourism with an evening out at the horse races in the western suburb of Agios Dometios. ⓔ Ippodromion Street ⓘ 22 78 27 27 ⓐ Race meetings most Wednesdays and Saturdays in summer and Wednesdays and Sundays in winter ⓘ Admission charge

State Collection of Contemporary Art ★
Modern paintings and sculptures by Cypriot artists. ⓔ Leoforos Stasinou and Kritis Street ⓘ 22 30 49 47 ⓐ Open Mon–Fri 10.00–16.45, Sat 10.00–12.45 ⓘ Admission free

SHOPPING

The main shopping district in the Old City is defined by Ledra Street and the parallel Onasagorou Street, as well as those streets that connect them. The trendiest is Stasikratous Street. Here you will find a good mix of upmarket and popular shops, with price tags to match. Outside the Venetian walls, the long Leoforos Archiepiskopou Makariou III has excellent shopping possibilities, with interesting boutiques in adjacent streets.

The best of Lefkosia is found in Laïki Geitonia, an enclave of atmospheric tavernas with street terraces, attractively restored old buildings, and craft and souvenir shops, all in a pleasant, though busy, pedestrians-only zone. ⓐ Between Ledra Street and Aischylou Street, adjacent to Eleftheria Plateia

Cyprus Handicraft Service
The best of traditional handmade Cyprus products are on sale at this government-owned foundation. Its products are labelled 'CHS' and include pottery, wood carvings, handmade lace, loom embroidery and cotton work. There is also a workshop and exhibition centre, where traditional craftspeople can be seen in action. ⓐ 186 Leoforos Athalassis, in the southern suburbs, close to the Larnaka motorway access ⓣ 22 30 50 24

Markets An outdoor fruit and vegetable market is held every Wednesday morning at the Constanza Bastion of the Venetian walls. There are also permanent municipal markets at Dimarchias Square in the Old City, and the junction of Leoforos Digeni Akrita with Leoforos Evgenias kai Antoniou Theodotou.

The Moufflon Probably the best English bookshop in Cyprus. They will search for, order and deliver books. A mine of local information. ⓐ 1 Sofouli Street ⓣ 22 66 51 55

LEFKOSIA

> **LEFKOSIA INTERNATIONAL AIRPORT**
> Cyprus's former international airport lies outside the city to the west. Caught in the middle of the 1974 conflict, it has been closed since then. It is now the main UN base in Cyprus. This situation could change, as reopening the airport is one of the 'confidence-building measures' proposed by the UN as a means of moving towards a solution. You can catch a glimpse of the place, complete with aircraft wrecked in the fighting, by driving out through the suburb of Egkomi on Leoforos Kyriakou Matsi or Leoforos Griva Digeni, but you will be stopped at a checkpoint before reaching it.

Tripiotis Church ★
A richly embellished 17th-century church that was the favoured place of worship of Lefkosia's leading citizens in its time. Franco-Byzantine in style. ❸ Solonos Street ❍ Open irregularly ❶ Admission free

Venetian Walls ★★★
Built by Cyprus's Venetian occupiers to defend against a long-awaited Ottoman invasion that finally came in 1570, the walls failed miserably to protect the city. The Turks stormed the walls and killed a reported 20,000 inhabitants. Still, the circular walls look strong enough even today and you can visit six of the eleven bastions that stand like gigantic pendants on the necklace of fortifications (the others are in the Turkish-occupied sector). Some sections of the moat have been laid out as gardens and make pleasant places for a stroll, especially during winter when they are filled with lush green grass and flowers. ❸ From the Pafos Gate to beyond the Famagusta Gate ❍ Open permanently ❶ Admission free

---

The Municipal Swimming Pool is a popular complex of outdoor pools where children can make a splash for hours at a time.
❸ Leoforos Louki Akrita ❍ Open daily in summer ❶ Admission charge

RESORTS

RESTAURANTS

Aegeon €€ ❶ Although restaurants and cafés in the Famagusta Gate area are generally smart, stylish and pricey, Aegeon has managed to resist the temptation to follow suit and has remained true to its roots as a family taverna with fine traditional cooking. ⓐ 40 Ektoros Street ⓣ 22 43 32 97

Arhondiko €€ ❷ On a summer evening this is a romantic place where you can eat out of doors, enveloped in the glow of lanterns, gently serenaded by Greek music. ⓐ 27 Aristokyprou Street, Laïki Geitonia ⓣ 22 68 00 80

Armenaki € ❸ As its name suggests, this is an Armenian restaurant, serving the finely cooked, lightly spiced food popular with this community in Cyprus – and with others who have acquired a taste for it. Although a simple restaurant, it is popular with Lefkosians of all social classes ⓐ 15 Sans Souci Street ⓣ 22 37 83 83

Erenias €€ ❹ Strovolos, once a village outside Lefkosia, has been swallowed up by the burgeoning capital. It's a bit out of town, but the trip is worth it, in particular for the *meze* served in surroundings of unpretentious charm. ⓐ 64a Leoforos Archiepiskopou Kyprianou, Strovolos ⓣ 22 42 28 60

Konatzin €€ ❺ Vegetarian restaurants are thin on the ground in Cyprus. Yet Konatzin serves a great vegetarian *meze* in the elegant setting of a converted town mansion with a garden terrace. ⓐ 10 Delfi Street ⓣ 22 77 69 90

Plaka Taverna €€ ❻ The tables of this taverna spread across a terrace among the flowers of the old village square. It is a great place to eat *meze*. ⓐ 8 Stylianou Lena Street, Egkomi ⓣ 22 35 28 98

LEFKOSIA

Get a bird's-eye view of Lefkosia from the top of the Ermes building

Xefoto €€ ❼ A step up from the standard fare in the Laïki Geitonia district, Xefoto has an outside terrace, a stylish café-restaurant on the ground floor and a more intimate spot upstairs. All three serve a well-prepared, modern interpretation of Cypriot cuisine. 6 Aischylou Street, Laïki Geitonia 22 66 65 67

NIGHTLIFE

There are a number of good cinemas, showing international films (mostly American) in their original language, with Greek subtitles. Among them is the **Zena Palace**, at Theofanos Theodotou Street near Eleftheria Plateia, with **Pantheon** and **Opera** cinemas close by.

If you want a telescope view of Lefkosia, visit the **Ledra Museum-Observatory** on the 11th floor of the Ermes department store at the corner of Ledra Street and Arsinoes Street.

AGIA NAPA

Agia Napa (Ayia Napa)
fun in the sun

Set in the red earth of the Kokkinochoria district north east of Larnaka, Agia Napa was once a sleepy fishing harbour dating back to 1366, but is now a modern beach resort built for fun in the sun. Its focal points are the bustling Seferi Plateia, the harbour and, of course, the beaches, some of which lie just outside the resort itself.

 Agia Napa's tourist information office is at Leoforos Kryou Nerou.
❶ 23 72 17 96

THINGS TO SEE & DO
Agia Napa Harbour and Marina ★★
Presents a busy and colourful scene of fishing boats, tour boats, glass-bottomed boats and private yachts. In front of the harbour, the tiny, whitewashed chapel of Agios Georgios looks out of place amid the tourist clutter. ❸ End of Leoforos Archiepiskopou Makariou III

Agia Thekla ★
A whitewashed chapel overlooking the sea near Nissi Bay. An older chapel, dug into the rocks nearby, has a few icons illuminated only by an oil lamp. ❸ Open permanently ❶ Admission free

Agia Napa Monastery ★
A cool and tranquil place to escape the crowds, with a pretty fountain, some shade-giving trees and a handful of ageing nuns in attendance.
❸ Beside Seferi Plateia ❸ Open dawn–dusk ❶ Admission free

Agii Anargyri ★★
A small chapel beside the sea north of Cape Greko, at the end of a rough track off the main road. Its dazzling white makes a nice contrast with the sea's deep blue. The sandy beach along a shallow bay a little further north is one of the best on this stretch of coast.

RESORTS

Cape Greko ★★★
This cape is at the tip of a long peninsula south east of Agia Napa, lined by dramatic cliffside scenery. An overlook that you can reach on foot from a parking area near the Cape gives a dramatic view along the rugged coastline towards Agia Napa. The Cape and the lighthouse at its tip are fenced off because of nearby military and civilian communications facilities. Experienced snorkellers and divers explore the waters around here – but it is no place for inexperienced amateurs.

Dhekelia ★
The barracks and headquarters of the British Sovereign Base, one of two in Cyprus (the other is at Episkopi/Akrotiri in the west). It is a very British residential area, with street names such as Waterloo Road.

Dinosaurs Park ★★
Family attraction with models of prehistoric creatures that lived millions of years ago, complete with sounds. ⓐ Off Leoforos Nissi ⓘ 22 84 32 23 ⓛ Open June–Nov 11.00–13.00 and 16.00–midnight

EMW Go-Karts ★★
A place for older children to test their skills on the circuit. ⓐ Agia Thekla Road (next to Water World). ⓘ 23 72 36 89 ⓛ Open 09.00–18.00 ⓘ Hire charge

Municipal Museum of Marine Life ★★
A new museum that takes as its theme the marine life around Cyprus's coast, with dioramas and exhibition cases. ⓐ Agia Napa Town Hall, 25 Agias Mavris Street ⓘ 23 72 34 09 ⓛ Open Mon–Fri 09.00–14.00, Sat 09.00–13.00 ⓘ Admission charge

Potamos Creek ★★
Small fishing boats crowd into this creek harbour near Liopetri village, creating a colourful and tranquil scene. The fishermen themselves eat in the two harbourside tavernas, where fish is fresh off the boats.

AGIA NAPA

 Cycle along the coastal road west from Makronissos beach for a much quieter route to the Potamos Creek fishing harbour.

Pyla ★
Greek and Turkish Cypriots still live in harmony in this village on the edge of Britain's Dhekelia Sovereign Base Area. There is an Orthodox church and a mosque, Turkish coffee shop and Greek *kafenion*, all watched over by UN peacekeepers. A 16th-century Venetian watchtower stands on the rugged Cape Pyla coast.

Water World Water Park ★★★
Kamikaze slides, river tube rides and rolling logs guarantee the children will be amused at this well-equipped aqua park. Adults can relax at the beach, or at the poolside bars and restaurants. ❸ Agia Thekla Road ❶ 23 72 44 44 Ⓦ www.waterworldwaterpark.com ❹ Open Apr–Nov 10.00–18.00 ❶ Admission charge

EXCURSION
Take a boat trip from the harbour along the coast to see the sad but fascinating sight of Varosha, a suburb of Famagusta that was once Cyprus's main tourist resort. Under Turkish occupation since 1974, it has been totally deserted and is literally crumbling to the ground.

RED EARTH
The countryside around Agia Napa is called the Kokkinochoria (Red Villages) district. Its irrigated red soil produces three crops a year of the Cyprus potatoes that are so popular in Britain. Not so long ago, windmills that used to draw water from underground sources were abandoned in favour of diesel pumps. Now, some of those once rusting windmills are being restored and brought back into use again, creating a handsome sight.

RESORTS

BEACHES
Agia Napa Beach ★★★
Very convenient beach on the bay east of the harbour. In two sections, Pethamenia and Kryo Nero, ending at the Thalassines Spilies (Sea Caves).

Makronissos Beach ★★★
The last in the chain of beaches west of Agia Napa, with an excavated warren of ancient Greek and Roman tombs, free and open to the public.

Nissi Beach ★★★
The best of a cluster of good – but very busy – beaches lying a few miles west of Agia Napa. Easily reachable by bus from the resort, there are good water sports and other beach facilities here.

RESTAURANTS

Esperia €€–€€€ ❶ Seafood is the speciality in this harbour taverna, which is virtually in the sea. The fish comes straight off the nearest fishing boat, and the menu includes kalamari and prawn dishes. ⓐ Agia Napa Harbour ⓣ 23 72 16 35

Jasmine Inn €€ ❷ A happy-go-lucky, popular British-style cocktail bar. Serves meals all day – breakfast, lunch and dinner. The party starts after 23.00 hours! ⓐ Dionysos Solomou Street ⓣ 23 72 17 31

Ji-Li €€ ❸ Serves authentic Chinese and Cantonese food in pretty, traditional surroundings. Has over 100 specialities on the menu, plus takeaway service. Friendly staff. ⓐ 48 Nissi Leoforos, on the junction of Agias Mavris Street ⓣ 23 72 20 22

Koutouki Tavern ❹ €€ A traditional Cypriot taverna known for its 20-dish *meze*. Original dishes as well as traditional Cypriot and international. Lots of fish. Nightly entertainment and dancing, plus a local history museum. ⓐ Leoforos Nissi (near the Sunwing Hotel) ⓣ 23 72 25 14

▲ *Nissi beach, near Agia Napa*

🍴 **Limelight Taverna** €€ ❺ Open since the 1980s, this taverna is one of the most popular in Agia Napa. Serves quality local produce in excellent surroundings. A sizzling suckling pig being cooked on an open rotisserie is a regular sight! 🅐 10 Lipertis Street 🅣 23 72 16 50

🍴 **Napa House Taverna** €€ ❻ Still one of the best tavernas in Agia Napa, with typical Cypriot fare that includes a fine *meze* as well as European dishes. A cosily romantic atmosphere inside, with an outside terrace. 🅐 Dimokratis Street 🅣 23 72 21 74

🍴 **Taverna Mangas** ❼ €€ Family-oriented to the extent of having a children's playground, Taverna Mangas serves international food and typical Cypriot dishes such as *meze*, *kleftiko* and *moussaka*, as well as fish. 🅐 Leoforos Nissi (opposite Sunwing Hotel) 🅣 23 72 29 76

🍴 **To Ploumin** €€ ❽ One of the area's best tavernas, in a 1930s village house decorated with traditional household and farming implements, and with a listed windmill. Home cooking uses fresh ingredients from surrounding farms. 🅐 3 Oktovriou 28 Street 🅣 23 73 01 44

NIGHTLIFE

A mecca for partygoers, Agia Napa boasts enough nightlife to make your head spin! Party in the central square at night, later following the crowds to popular haunts **Carwash**, **Moods** and **River Reggae**.

RESORTS

Protaras
ruggedly beautiful coast

Along with the related resort of Pernera, Protaras occupies the furthest south-eastern corner of Cyprus accessible to visitors. A little further up the road is the UN buffer zone. It is a purpose-built family resort area, quieter than Agia Napa, and specializes in getting the maximum of holiday fun out of sun, sea and sand. Along this ruggedly beautiful stretch of coastline there used to be nothing except a few fishing harbours and some little country churches.

THINGS TO SEE & DO
You'll see just about everything there is to do in Protaras as soon as you look out of your hotel room window in the morning at the sun rising out of the sea. The thing to do here is to head for the beach. In addition, there are some easy bicycle or walking trips to make, in and around the resort, including to Paralimni and Agias Trias harbours to see the fishing boats, and to Profitis Ilias Church, not so much for the little church itself as for the view from the hill on which it stands.

◐ *Fig Tree Bay*

PROTARAS

Ammochostos (Famagusta) viewpoints ★
There are several places around Dherynia from where you can view the abandoned city of Famagusta. Annita's View Point is a popular location, and provides binoculars and information. Famagusta Beach View and the Cultural Centre of Occupied Famagusta are two more. You can take a visual 'tour' of Varosha, a crumbling and deserted suburb of Famagusta that was once Cyprus's main tourist resort. Varosha can also be visited by boat (see page 29).

Water sports ★
Being the main attraction of the resorts, the beaches in the area of Protaras, Pernera, Fig Tree Bay and Konnos Bay have a full range of water sports facilities.

EXCURSIONS
Agia Trias ★
North of Pernera, a side road to the right off the main coast road leads to a pleasant sandy bay and a cluster of seaside tavernas beside a small chapel.

Dheryneia ★★
This inland village is jammed up against the demarcation line. From the Viewpoint Café's observation tower you can look with binoculars and a telescope across the UN buffer zone to the Turkish-occupied part of Cyprus, in the direction of the abandoned and crumbling resort of Varosha, near Famagusta.

Paralimni ★
A big village that offers some traditional Cypriot character in an area that is otherwise notable only for its tourist resorts. The main square consists of a cluster of impressive churches surrounded by cafés and tavernas. West of the town is Paralimni Lake, which fills up with water during winter and dries out to a muddy swamp in summer.

RESORTS

> **SHOPPING**
> **GT** For good quality Italian leather goods at factory prices, on Hotel Road, near the Sunrise Hotel. ☏ 23 83 12 24
> **La Lenia** For ladies' fashion accessories, jewellery, leather goods, watches, perfumes, etc. The company has four different boutiques in Protaras, all on Hotel Road. ☏ 23 83 22 70

Profitis Ilias ★
Midway between Protaras and Pernera, on the left side of the road, this small and handsome church commands a fine view of the coast.

> Cycle or drive to Cape Greko, an area of great natural beauty between Protaras and Agia Napa, and easily reached. This will get you away from the summer beach crowds, and you will find plenty of sheltered coves for swimming and snorkelling, as well as shaded walks along the nature trails of the Cape Greko Forest Park.

BEACHES
Konnos Beach ★★★
Lying south east of Protaras, at the edge of the scenic Cape Greko area, the facilities include sunbeds, beach umbrellas, pedalos and paragliding. Accessible by bus from Protaras.

Pernera Beach ★★★
Pernera is a northward extension of Protaras, separated from it by a zone of citrus orchards and connected by road.

Protaras Beach and Fig Tree Bay ★★★
These two stretches of beach run into each other along the front of Protaras, and are reached by several side roads.

PROTARAS

RESTAURANTS

Anatolia €€ Despite its Turkish-sounding name, this is a Greek Cypriot taverna, serving excellent food, which specializes in that most Cypriot of meals, the many small dishes of a *meze* – a great way to sample the traditional fare. It also offers international dishes.
ⓐ Agios Elias ❶ 23 83 15 33

Il Cavaliere €€ One of the oldest established Italian restaurants in Protaras. This place serves fine pasta, meat, and fish dishes, and has a vegetarian menu, plus Italian wines and ice creams. ⓐ In Pernera, just off the main strip in Protaras ❶ 23 83 10 22

Dragon No 2 €€ All your favourite Chinese dishes can be found on the menu of this popular and friendly restaurant, where the prices will not leave a large hole in your pocket. ⓐ Protaras Road ❶ 23 83 14 14

Sao Paulo €€ For something truly unique, try this family restaurant serving great Brazilian and Italian cuisine – the only one of its kind in Cyprus! Sea view and special children's menus.
ⓐ Hotel Road ❶ 23 83 26 10

Spartiatis €€ This restaurant specializes in seafood fresh from the nearby harbour and traditional Greek dishes, serving it all up in a quiet, romantic atmosphere. ⓐ Konnos beach
❶ 23 83 13 86

NIGHTLIFE

Protaras boasts a number of bars, pubs and clubs, including the longest running and most popular nightclub in the area, **Boogies Disco**. Its **Sfinx Bar** is legendary. Other favourites for partying include the clubs **Return of the Kings**, **Knights** and **Niata**.

RESORTS

Larnaka (Larnaca)
palm-fringed bay

The third-biggest town in Cyprus, with a population of some 60,000, Larnaka is a busy commercial centre as well as being a holiday resort. There are plenty of visitor attractions in the centre and a reasonable beach adjoining the seafront promenade. Other beach and water sports facilities lie outside town to the south and the east, along Larnaka Bay.

Larnaka has two tourist information offices: **Airport tourist office** ⓐ International Airport ⓘ 24 64 35 76; and **Cyprus Tourist Organisation office** ⓐ Vasileos Pavlou Plateia ⓘ 24 65 43 22. Every Wednesday at 10.00 hours, there is a free walking tour of Larnaka: 'Larnaka Past and Present', starting at the Cyprus Tourist Organisation office at Vasileos Pavlou Plateia on the seafront. Every Friday at 10.00 hours, there is a free tour of the craft district of Scala, beginning at Larnaka Fort ⓘ 24 65 43 22

THINGS TO SEE & DO
Agia Faneromeni ★
An underground chapel in a cavern that is thought to have been a pagan tomb dating back to Phoenician times. Now dedicated to a Christian saint, it is a local place of pilgrimage, visited by sick people and by girls whose lovers are overseas. ⓐ Leoforos Faneromenis ⓛ Open permanently ⓘ Admission free

Agios Lazaros Church ★
The 17th-century Orthodox church has a beautiful gilded iconostasis (altar screen) and the sepulchre of St Lazarus, who was raised from the dead by Jesus. There is also a small Byzantine museum in the church grounds, showing icons and other religious items. ⓐ Agiou Lazarou Street ⓛ Open 08.30–12.30 and 15.30–18.30 (Apr–Aug); 08.00–12.30 and 14.30–17.00 (Sept–Mar) ⓘ Admission free

Ancient Kition ★

Birthplace of the philosopher Zeno, ancient Kition has almost entirely vanished, thanks to the British, who carted away most of the ruins during the 19th century for use as building materials in Egypt. In this once important Phoenician, Greek and Roman city, you can just about identify the straggly remains of a Phoenician temple to the goddess Astarte, which burned down in 312 BC. A stele (grave marker) found on the site (now in a Berlin museum) carries an inscription boasting of the power of the Assyrian King Sargon II, who conquered Cyprus in 709 BC.

ⓐ Off Leontiou Machaira Street ⓛ Open Mon–Fri 09.00–14.30 (and Thurs 15.00–17.00, except July and Aug) ⓘ Admission charge

Cami Kebir (Grand Mosque) ★

The mosque is still used by local and visiting Muslims, but you can usually visit it, and stroll for a while through its peaceful interior.

ⓐ Beside Larnaka Fort, on Phinikoudes Beach ⓛ Open daily
ⓘ Admission free (but a donation is welcome)

RESORTS

Kamares Aqueduct ★
Altogether 33 arches survive from this aqueduct, south west of Larnaka, built by the Ottomans in the 18th century to bring water to Larnaka from the Troodos foothills. ⓐ Beside the Larnaka–Lemesos Road on the edge of the city (see also page 71)

Hala Sultan Tekke ★★★
This mosque nestles in a grove of palm trees by the shore of Larnaka's Salt Lake. Although it dates from the early 19th century, it incorporates the tomb of the Hala Sultan, also known as Umm Haram, a relative of the Prophet Mohammed, who died in Cyprus in AD 649. The sepulchre is covered in green cloths of mourning (see page 72). ⓛ Open 07.30–19.30 (summer); 09.00–17.00 (winter); 09.00–18.00 (spring and autumn) ⓘ Admission free (but a donation is welcome)

Larnaka District Archaeological Museum ★★
This museum houses a selection of pottery, coins, bronzes and statuary, with a noteworthy collection from nearby historic sites such as Kition and Choirokoitia. ⓐ Kalograion Plateia, near Larnaka Tennis Club ⓣ 24 30 41 69 ⓛ Open Mon–Fri 09.00–14.30, also Thurs 15.00–17.00 (except during summer) ⓘ Admission charge

Larnaka Fort ★★★
The 17th-century Larnaka Fort occupies a dramatic position overlooking the sea and houses a medieval museum, displaying suits of armour and other historical objects. ⓐ Phinikoudes Promenade ⓣ 24 30 45 76 ⓛ Open 09.00–19.00 (summer); 09.00–17.00 (winter); 09.00–18.00 (spring and autumn), closed Sat and Sun ⓘ Admission charge

Marina ★★
In Larnaka Marina, cabin-cruisers, yachts, glass-bottomed cruise boats and excursion cruisers are lined up side by side. ⓐ Beside Vasileos Pavlou Plateia

Larnaka promenade

Municipal Museum of Palaeontology ★★
Just the thing for children who can't get enough of dinosaurs. Housed in five former Customs stores that date back to the period of British rule in the early 19th century. ⓐ Municipal Cultural Centre, Europa Plateia ⓘ 24 62 85 87 ⓞ Open Tues–Fri 09.00–14.00, Sat and Sun 09.00–noon (closed Sun, Mon in June–Aug) ⓘ Admission free

Municipal Park ★★
Larnaka, like other Cypriot towns, is short of green spaces, which makes this small triangle of trees, plants and grass in the town centre a doubly welcome source of shade on a hot, dusty day. The Municipal Library and Natural History Museum stand in the grounds. ⓐ Leoforos Grigori Afxentiou ⓞ Open permanently ⓘ Admission free

Natural History Museum ★★
Scenes from the natural world in Cyprus, such as pink flamingos in the Salt Lakes at Larnaka and the Akrotiri Peninsula. ⓐ Leoforos Grigori Afxentiou (situated inside Larnaka Municipal Park) ⓘ 24 65 25 69 ⓞ Open Tues–Sun 10.00–13.00 and 16.00–18.00 (June–Aug); 10.00–13.00 and 15.00–17.00 (Sept–May), closed Mon ⓘ Admission charge

RESORTS

Phinikoudes Promenade ★★★
This is a handsome stretch of walkway along the seafront from the Marina almost as far as Larnaka Fort, and decorated with ornamental street-lamps and palm trees. Beside it are smart, open-air cafés and restaurants. A bust of the ancient Athenian hero Kimon, who lost his life in an unsuccessful attempt to free the city from the Persians, stands on the promenade.

Pierides Foundation Archaeological Museum ★★
A private archaeological museum that is operated by the Pierides Foundation, housed in a 19th-century mansion. It displays pottery, glassware, ornaments and statues from the Stone Age to the end of the Roman Empire. ⓐ 4 Zinonos Kitieos Street ⓣ 24 81 45 55 ⓞ Open Mon–Thurs 09.00–16.00, Fri and Sat 09.00–13.00, closed Sun ⓘ Admission charge

BEACHES
While there is a reasonable beach on the Larnaka seafront, most of the coastal action in town takes place along curving Larnaka Bay on the Larnaka to Dhekelia road. In addition to a long stretch of beach, lined with a full range of water sports possibilities, there are cafés, restaurants and shops.

RESTAURANTS

Alakati €–€€ ❶ Specializing in big platefuls of Cypriot food, this simple seafront taverna is popular with Cypriot families and with tourists who appreciate hearty Cypriot cooking. ⓐ 7 Ankara Street ⓣ 24 65 30 42

Archontiko €€ ❷ This restaurant is situated in a picturesque old building beside the Phinikoudes Promenade, with seafront views. The traditional Cypriot food is very good, and the associated Archontissa is an equally good steakhouse. ⓐ 24 Leoforos Athinon ⓣ 24 65 59 05

SHOPPING

 Cyprus Handicraft Service The only Larnaka branch of the government-operated handicrafts foundation.
📍 6 Kosma Lysioti Street ☎ 24 30 43 27

Fruit market Located in the middle of the old Turkish quarter, this small but busy fruit and vegetable market is worth a visit.
📍 Ermou Street

Laïki Geitonia (Geitonia) Arts and crafts and good souvenir shops. 📍 One street behind the seafront, near the Larnaka Fort

Tofarides Bookshop Books in English and other languages, along with cards and more. 📍 45–47 Zinonos Street
☎ 24 65 49 12

Masalas €€–€€€ ❸ An excellent Indian restaurant with an outdoor terrace and darkly atmospheric interior. Though the menu is relatively short, the dishes are carefully prepared, with prompt and friendly service. 📍 Larnaka–Dhekelia Road ☎ 24 64 49 50

Monte Carlo €€ ❹ A stylish restaurant with a balcony overlooking the Mediterranean in the old Turkish quarter of Larnaka. 📍 28 Pigale Pasha Street ☎ 24 65 38 15

Panos Steak House €€ ❺ A straightforward restaurant that does more than steaks, having traditional Cypriot food and seafood dishes on the menu. The roof garden terrace overlooking the sea is a big draw. 📍 Ankara Street, near Larnaka Fort ☎ 24 65 37 07

Pyla Fish Tavern €€ ❻ This is one of the oldest fish taverns in Larnaka. It has a very good reputation and offers a large selection of fresh fish dishes as well as traditional Cypriot cooking.
📍 Larnaka–Dhekelia Road ☎ 24 64 59 90

RESORTS

Lemesos (Limassol)
the island's second city

Cyprus's second largest city, after Lefkosia, Lemesos (also known as Limassol) combines an industrial and shipping role with that of a seaside resort. There are plenty of things to see and do, and an active dining, nightlife and cultural scene, although it lacks some of the family-oriented facilities of dedicated beach resorts, such as Agia Napa.

Lemesos has three tourist information offices:
Downtown office ⓐ 115A Spyrou Araouzou Street ⓣ 25 36 27 56
Germasogeia office ⓐ 22 Georgiou A' Street ⓣ 25 32 32 11
Lemesos harbour office ⓣ 25 57 18 68

THINGS TO SEE & DO
Archaeological Museum ★
Houses many important finds from the ancient Greek and Roman cities of Amathous and Kourion that lie close to Lemesos. Among the treasures are statues of Aphrodite and of Egyptian and Phoenician gods.
ⓐ Kanningos and Vyronos Street ⓣ 25 30 51 57 ⓒ Open Mon–Fri 09.00–17.00, Sat 10.00–13.00, closed Sun ⓘ Admission charge

Boat tours ★
Take cruises from Lemesos Old Harbour, around Akrotiri Peninsula, to Pissouri beach and view the Rock of Aphrodite. Several tour companies also operate glass-bottomed boats.

Folk Art Museum ★★
Mementoes of a mostly vanished Cypriot lifestyle, in a 19th-century mansion, including all kinds of work and household objects and furnishings that were in use until recent times. ⓐ 253 Agiou Andreou Street ⓣ 25 36 23 03 ⓒ Open 08.30–13.30 and 16.00–18.30 (June–Sept); 15.00–17.30 (Oct–May), closed Thur afternoon, and Sat and Sun ⓘ Admission charge

RESORTS

WATER PARKS
Several water parks, all with lifeguards, have opened recently in Lemesos, adding a new dimension to family fun in the resort.

Fassouri Watermania
On 17 hectares (42 acres), with a huge wave pool, water slides that include a kamikaze slide, a Lazy River, adult and children's pools, restaurant, cafeteria and snack bars. ⓐ Trahoni Village Road ⓘ 25 71 42 35 ⓐ www.watermania-fasouri.com ⓒ Open May–Oct 10.00–18.00 ⓘ Admission charge

Wet 'n' Wild
Tubes, slides, pools, swim-up bar and restaurants. ⓐ Junction 23 (Mouttagiaka exit) on the A1 motorway ⓘ 25 31 80 00 ⓐ www.wetnwild.com.cy ⓒ Open April–Oct 10.00–18.00 ⓘ Admission charge

Lemesos Castle and Cyprus Medieval Museum ★★★
The castle is a battlemented affair that was originally built during the Crusader era in the 12th century by the Lusignan kings. Venetians, Turks and the British all added bits and pieces to it and changed others. Nowadays the arched stone halls in its interior house the Cyprus Medieval Museum, displaying weapons, sculptures and other items from that period. ⓐ Off Eirinis Street near the Old Harbour ⓘ 25 30 54 19 ⓒ Open Mon–Sat 09.00–17.00, Sun 10.00–13.00 ⓘ Admission charge

Old Harbour ★★
This is Lemesos's more human-scale fishing and yacht harbour, from which the coastal tour boats leave. It is located near the castle, at the end of the seafront promenade.

LEMESOS

Time Elevator ★★

A thrilling attraction where visitors 'travel' through time to experience events in Cyprus's history. ❷ Behind Lemesos Castle ❶ 25 76 28 28 ❿ Open 09.20–20.40 (summer); 09.15–18.15 (winter) ❶ Admission charge

Turkish Quarter ★★

When you come out of Lemesos Castle you are in the old Turkish quarter of the city. It is well worth strolling around its narrow streets for an hour. Among Turkish Cypriot monuments in this area are the Djami Kebir Mosque, the Köprülü Haji Ibrahim Mosque and a Turkish bath-house. Some of the elegant Ottoman-style houses have Turkish inscriptions.

BEACHES

Lemesos Beach runs more or less the full length of Lemesos's seafront adjoining Oktovriou 28 Street. It has loungers, beach umbrellas and pedalos.

RESTAURANTS & BARS

Akti Olous €€ ❶ With an outside terrace overlooking the sea, this is a great place to eat the house speciality: *meze*, either meat or seafood. There are other dishes as well, such as *stifado*, *kleftiko* and steak. ❷ Galatex Beach Centre, Potamos Germasogeias ❶ 25 31 44 04

Aliada €€ ❷ A cosy restaurant in a beautifully restored house, this place has an extensive menu of local produce, home-made soups, a great cold buffet and charcoaled meat and fish. ❷ 117 Eirinis Street ❶ 25 34 07 58

Blue Island €€–€€€ ❸ For a special evening out, this is one of the classiest restaurants in the Lemesos area, serving French and international cuisine in a somewhat formal setting. There is a shaded, vine-covered patio/garden for outdoor dining. ❷ 3 Leoforos Amathountos, Old Lemesos–Lefkosia Road ❶ 25 32 14 66

SHOPPING

Bustling and cosmopolitan Lemesos has plenty of shopping, dining-out and nightlife opportunities. Most of these are situated conveniently within the relatively small city centre and along the seafront, although others are in the nearby resort suburb of Germasogeias.

Cyprus Handicraft Service The only Lemesos branch of the government-operated handicrafts foundation. ⓐ 25 Themidos Street ⓣ 25 30 51 18

Markets There are two fruit and vegetable markets, both of them located near the Cyprus Tourism Organisation office. ⓐ Genethliou Mitella Street and Saripolou Street

Marks & Spencer Do not expect the full range of goods found in the big British stores of this UK-based firm – but you will find good-quality clothes – including M & S's excellent underwear. ⓐ Leoforos Nykiforou Grigora ⓣ 25 74 81 66

Monte Napoleone Boutique Upmarket women's fashions from the likes of Gianfranco Ferre, Thierry Mugler and others. ⓐ 90 Leoforos Griva Digeni ⓣ 25 58 97 25

Ermes (formerly Woolworth) A well-known department store chain throughout Cyprus that offers an upmarket selection of goods, its prices remain keen and the store is popular with locals and tourists alike. Best buys include clothes, cosmetics, food and ceramics souvenirs. Lemesos has two branches: ⓐ Ermes Apollon, Petrou Tsirou Street ⓣ 25 83 18 31; ⓐ Ermes Olympia, Oktovriou 28 Street ⓣ 25 59 11 33

LEMESOS

▲ *The Church of Agia Triada, Lemesos*

Captain Cook €–€€ ❹ Traditional Cypriot menu offered plus some international dishes. Outside seating in the summer and a relaxed family atmosphere. ⓐ 58a Georgiou A' Street ⓣ 25 32 57 49

Chef Peking €€ ❺ A top-quality Chinese restaurant serving a wide range of dishes, such as chicken chow mein, sweet and sour pork and beef in black-bean sauce. ⓐ Sun Sea Court, Block 1 (Trans Hotel), Leoforos Amathous ⓣ 25 31 48 28

Hamlet € ❻ An English-style pub with a friendly, relaxed, family atmosphere. Bar snacks are also served. ⓐ 72b Leoforos Amathous ⓣ 25 32 08 52

RESORTS

Lucky Leprechaun € ❼ There are no prizes for guessing that this is an Irish bar, but the place is a bit of a prize in itself. As well as a range of Irish beers, it has karaoke evenings and a big-screen television for major sporting events. ⓐ Galatex Beach Centre, Potomos Germasogeias ❶ 25 31 42 18

Neo Phaliro €€ ❽ Highly regarded by local diners for its excellent local and international food and uncompromising Cypriot character. ⓐ 135 Gladstonos Street ❶ 25 36 57 68

Porta €€ ❾ How do you feel about eating in a renovated donkey stable? Designer class and good taste characterize this restaurant in the old Turkish quarter. ⓐ 17 Genethliou Mitella Street ❶ 25 36 03 39

Scotties Steakhouse €€ ❿ This restaurant specializes in steaks – good ones – making this a popular place. ⓐ 38 Souliou Street ❶ 25 57 51 73

Ship Inn € ⓫ If you need your full British breakfast and familiar dishes for lunch and dinner, this is a good place to go. The sea view adds atmosphere to what is already a family-oriented and friendly place. ⓐ Kerkyra Street ❶ 25 58 21 80

Taj Mahal €€ ⓬ Excellent service and authentic Indian food. Every item on the menu is good, with the chicken korma and chicken tikka masala winning especially favourable notices. ⓐ Viotias and Trapezoundos Streets, Potomos Germasogeias ❶ 25 32 65 00

Tepee Rock Club €€ ⓭ An unusual and lively restaurant with displays of rock memorabilia. Great fun. A menu of hot Mexican dishes. ⓐ Ambelikon Road, Potomos Yermasoyias ❶ 25 32 82 22

LEMESOS

● *Lemesos – a bustling shipping city*

Trata €€ ⑭ A family-run restaurant that serves excellent *mezes* of fish straight from the boats. All at a good price. ⓐ 4 Ioanni Tompazi Street, Ermes Olympia complex ⓣ 25 58 66 00

Xydas €€€ ⑮ First-class seafood restaurant that serves fresh (as opposed to frozen) fish. ⓐ 22 Anthemidos Street, Amathous ⓣ 25 72 83 36

Yildizlar €€ ⑯ Fine Lebanese cuisine. ⓐ Leoforos Amathous, near turning for Agios Tychon ⓣ 25 32 27 55

NIGHTLIFE

Lemesos's extended seafront is the place to go for pubs, clubs and bars. Whether you're in the mood for robust partying or for a quiet drink with the family, you'll find the perfect place somewhere along this lively stretch. Many bars also show live international sporting events on a big screen.

RESORTS

Pafos (Paphos)
ancient Greek and Roman capital

Pafos is the least developed of the main resort areas on Cyprus, although that situation is changing fast. The lower town – Kato Pafos – has no shortage of eating and nightlife venues. Upper Pafos, known as Ktima, is more traditionally Cypriot. The town was the Cypriot capital under the ancient Greeks and Romans and it therefore has a rich collection of historic sites.

There are three tourist information offices in Pafos: 3 Gladstonos Street ❶ 26 93 28 41; 63 Leoforos Poseidonos, Kato Pafos ❶ 26 93 05 21; and at Pafos Airport ❶ 26 42 31 61

PAFOS

THINGS TO SEE & DO
Agia Solomoni Catacomb ★
This gloomy underground cavern was a refuge for persecuted Christians in ancient times. Local people believe that the tree beside the entrance, festooned with colourful votive cloths, is holy and can cure illness. ⓐ Leoforos Apostolou Pavlou ⓛ Open permanently ⓘ Admission free

Agios Neofytos Monastery ★
This shrine to the 12th-century Cypriot hermit St Neofytos, who carved a sanctuary (*egkleistra*) into the cliffside, is a popular place of pilgrimage. You can climb a stairway to see a small church in a cave that is decorated with murals. ⓐ Near Tala village, north of Pafos ⓛ Open 09.00–noon and 14.00–16.00 (Apr–Oct); 09.00–16.00 (Nov–Mar) ⓘ Admission charge

Archaeological Museum ★
Displays finds from the many local historical sites, such as the Tombs of the Kings. These include pottery, sculpture, coins and jewellery. A set of clay hot-water bottles shows that the ancient Romans found Cyprus chilly in winter. ⓐ Leoforos Georgiou Griva Digeni ⓘ 26 30 62 15 ⓛ Open Mon–Fri 09.00–17.00, Sat 10.00–13.00, closed Sun ⓘ Admission charge

Saranta Kolones (Byzantine Castle) ★
Built during the 12th century on the foundations of an earlier Byzantine fortification, this Crusader-era castle fell down during an earthquake shortly after it was completed. ⓐ Saranta Kolonon Street ⓛ Open dawn–dusk ⓘ Admission free

Byzantine Museum ★
This museum houses a collection of paintings and religious objects that include important 12th-century icons. ⓐ Andrea Ioannis Street ⓘ 26 93 13 93 ⓛ Open Mon–Fri 09.00–16.00, Sat 09.00–13.00 ⓘ Admission charge

RESORTS

Ethnographical Museum ★★
This museum contains pieces ranging from neolithic tools and ancient funerary sculptures, to traditional local costumes and everyday household objects. ⓐ 1 Exo Vrysis Street ⓣ 26 93 20 10 ⓛ Open Mon–Sat 09.00–17.00, Sun 10.00–13.00 ⓘ Admission charge

Geroskipou ★★
This village south east of Pafos has a long association with the myth of Aphrodite, the Greek goddess of love, as this is where she was said to have had her secret garden. In later times it became a silk-making centre of the Byzantine Empire after Orthodox monks smuggled some silk worms out of China. Now a busy suburb of Pafos, it is noted for a slew of pottery workshops along the main street, and shops selling Cypriot Delight (more commonly known in other countries as Turkish Delight). Geroskipou's tourist district runs along the seafront from Pafos, and is really an extension of the bigger town's hotels and beach zone. There's also a Museum of Folk Art and the old, five-domed Agia Paraskevi Byzantine Church.

Odeon ★
Ruins of Pafos's Greek theatre from the 2nd century AD, at the heart of an archaeological zone that includes the not easily recognizable remains of the ancient city's *agora* (marketplace) and a temple to Asklipeios, the god of healing. ⓐ Open 08.00–17.00 ⓘ Admission free (except during the Kourion Drama Festival – see page 79)

Pafos Aquarium ★★★
With lots of display tanks, the aquarium puts on a fine underwater show of marine life from the world's oceans and rivers. Stars of the display are sharks, crocodiles and piranhas, but less dangerous and more colourful creatures also have a place. ⓐ Artemidos I, Kato Pafos ⓣ 26 95 39 20 ⓛ Open 09.00–20.00 (summer); 09.00–19.00 (winter) ⓘ Admission charge

○ Roman mosaics at Pafos

Pafos Harbour ★★★
Filled with colourful fishing boats and tour boats, the harbour is lined with tavernas which – although not the best in Pafos – are popular and atmospheric. You can still see the ancient breakwaters, inside which Greek and Roman vessels once sheltered.

Pafos Fort ★★
Built by the Ottomans, this fort stands on the harbour wall, on the site of earlier castles dating back to ancient times. ⓐ Pafos harbour ⓑ Open 10.00–18.00 (summer); 10.00–17.00 (winter) ⓘ Admission charge

Pafos Mosaics ★★★
Located in a cluster of buildings dating from the Roman period, these mosaics are a major historical treasure. The House of Dionysos has scenes from pagan mythology; the House of Orpheus has a mosaic showing Orpheus playing his lyre; the Villa of Theseus is named after a mosaic showing Theseus battling with the Minotaur, and may have been the Roman governor's palace; and the House of Aion has superb mosaics of Greek deities. ⓐ Behind Pafos harbour ⓒ 26 30 62 17 ⓑ Open 08.00–17.00 (until 19.30 in summer) ⓘ Admission charge

SHOPPING

The upper town, Ktima, has the best shopping although there are plenty of souvenir shops in Kato Pafos.

Athos Diamond Centre This is certainly one of the best jewellery shops in Pafos, with a big selection, good quality, reasonable prices and helpful staff. ⓐ 79–80 Lighthouse Court, Leoforos Poseidonos, Kato Pafos ⓣ 26 81 16 30

Cyprus Handicraft Service A branch of this government-operated foundation. ⓐ 64 Leoforos Apostolou Pavlou ⓣ 26 30 62 43

Market Pafos market is small but makes up for this in atmosphere and bustle, and is surrounded by a shopping area. This is the place for souvenirs, lace and leather goods, as well as for fruit and vegetables and fresh seafood. ⓐ Junction of Nikodimou Mylona Street with Leoforos Archiepiskopou Makariou III ⓛ Open Mon–Sat (except Wed afternoon)

Marks & Spencer Focuses on clothes in contrast to the wider range found in Britain, but the goods are of the usual high quality. ⓐ Nikodimou Mylona Street ⓣ 26 22 27 71

Moufflon Bookshop One of the best bookshops for English and international books. ⓐ 30 Kinyras Street ⓣ 26 23 48 50

Ermes (formerly Woolworth) A well-known department store chain with an upmarket selection of goods, but prices are keen and the store is popular. Best buys include clothes, cosmetics, food and ceramic souvenirs. ⓐ Ermes Kinyras, Ledra Street, Kato Pafos ⓣ 26 94 71 22 ⓐ Ermes Korivos, Leoforos Dimokratia 2, Near Geroskipou ⓣ ⓣ 26 84 08 40

St Paul's Pillar ★

Panagia Chrysopolitissa church stands on the ruins of an early Christian basilica, containing a pillar where St Paul is said to have been scourged. Nearby Agia Solomoni Catacomb, a mysterious underground chamber, was a refuge for early Christians. ⓐ Leoforos Agiou Pavlou, Kato Pafos ⓑ The site of St Paul's Pillar is often closed for excavations ⓘ Admission free

Snake George (Reptile Park) ★

Something a little different for a family outing. Home to more than 100 snakes and other reptiles native to Cyprus. ⓐ Near junction of Agios Georgios Road, Pegeia ⓣ 99 98 76 85 ⓑ Open 10.00–sunset ⓘ Admission charge

Tombs of the Kings ★★

Dating from the 4th century BC, this is a complex of rock-cut tombs beside the sea, in which the leading citizens of Pafos (rather than kings) were buried. Carved steps lead down to the burial chambers and archaeologists are still uncovering more graves. ⓐ Tombs of the Kings (Tafoi ton Vasileon) Road ⓣ 26 30 62 95 ⓑ Open 08.00–19.30 (summer); 08.00–17.00 (winter); 08.00–18.00 (spring and autumn) ⓘ Admission charge

---

A great dining-out experience is an evening trip to nearby Pegeia village, which has a constellation of excellent village tavernas with outdoor terraces, all of which offer very good value. Unfortunately, the bus service to Pegeia is minimal even in summer, so it may have to be a car or taxi trip.

BEACHES

There are several small beaches on the seafront along Poseidonos Avenue, and bigger ones a mile or two south of town at Geroskipou. One of the best beaches in the area is at Coral Bay, 9.5 km (6 miles) north of Pafos and connected by a regular bus service.

RESORTS

RESTAURANTS & BARS

Cavallini €€–€€€ ❶ This is an excellent Italian restaurant with an upmarket approach and fine cooking. The atmosphere is relaxed and friendly. The fettucini in cream sauce with salmon strips is excellent, but there are plenty of other fine dishes to choose from. 65 Leoforos Poseidonos (between the Amathous Hotel and Rania Apartments) 26 96 41 64

Demokritos €€ ❷ Kato Pafos's oldest taverna (dating from 1971) adds traditional Greek and Cypriot dances and live music to its evening menu, making dinner something of a spectacle. The atmosphere is as lively as you would expect and food quality is up there with it. 1 Dionysos Street, Kato Pafos 26 93 33 71

Dos Pesos €€ ❸ Mexican restaurant that puts a full range of spicy food on the table and combines it with a lively, friendly atmosphere. Fajitas are the house speciality, and a range of Mexican and Spanish beers is served. Children's dishes are listed on the 'little hombres' menu. Tombs of the Kings (Tafoi ton Vasileon) Road 26 94 99 46

Fettas Corner €€ ❹ One of Pafos's little secrets, a place that Cypriots like to keep for themselves. A back-street location is the disguise for some of the best Cypriot cooking in town. 33 Ioannis Agrotis Street 26 93 78 22

Hollywood ❺ A good example of a dedicated cocktail bar. No food, no happy hour (all prices are reasonable) and no live music – just cocktails. 25 Agiou Antoniou Street, Kato Pafos 26 93 13 32

Pegasus Bar and Grill €€ ❻ A wooden interior and classic design identify this as an English-style pub, with a friendly staff and good snack food as well as a range of British beers. It also boasts an extensive cocktail menu. Blue Horizon, Block C7, Leoforos Danaes, Kato Pafos 26 96 4 9 09

🔺 *Pafos harbour*

🍴 **Pentaras** €€ ❼ An unremarkable taverna that nevertheless puts on a great evening of Cypriot and Greek dancing every Thursday, along with an all-you-can-eat buffet, with a summer terrace. You may find that there are more local people there than tourists. ⓐ Tombs of the Kings (Tafoi ton Vasileon) Road ⓘ 26 27 11 30

🍴 **Phuket** €€ ❽ A great Oriental restaurant serving traditional delicacies, including a good range of vegetarian dishes. ⓐ 44 Tombs of the Kings (Tafoi ton Vasileon) Road ⓘ 26 93 67 38

☕ **Tea For Two** € ❾ A home from home for those seeking British food, with items such as a full English breakfast, and Cornish pasty with chips, peas and gravy. They also do a takeaway service. ⓐ Tombs of the Kings (Tafoi ton Vasileon) Road ⓘ 26 93 78 95

NIGHTLIFE

Pafos has a good selection of pubs and clubs for evening entertainment. Among the most popular are **Aces Cocktail Bar**, **Dubbles Cocktail Bar** and **California Beach Bar**, all in Agios Antonios Street (otherwise known as Bar Street), Kato Pafos. **Boogies** ❿ is a bar-disco that lets visitors provide the live music by way of karaoke. It attracts a mix of local people and tourists. ⓐ Agiou Antoniou Street, Kato Pafos ⓘ 26 94 48 10 ⓞ Open 21.00–03.00

RESORTS

Coral Bay & Pegeia
golden sands and old village charm

Coral Bay is simply the best beach between Pafos and Latsi (Latchi), with golden sands and a sheltered bay that is ideal for children. The sun gets fierce here in summer but you can retreat to the shelter of one of the two beach cafés. Pegeia is the main settlement in the area surrounding Coral Bay, connected to it by a growing network of holiday and residential villas. Pegeia's main attraction lies in its old village charm. The centre is marked by the Orthodox church and a fountain popularized in a Cypriot folk song.

🔺 *Golden sands at Coral Bay*

CORAL BAY & PEGEIA

From here you can walk a few kilometres uphill to the Pegeia Forest. The expanding view as you climb the hill is well worth the effort. After this you can retire to one of the many excellent village tavernas for lunch or dinner.

THINGS TO SEE & DO
There are ancient ruins on the Maa headland that are worth looking at. Otherwise a walk along the cliffs on either side of Coral Bay, or a stroll among the nearby vineyards, orchards and banana plantations is the only alternative to the beach. Combined with a visit to a café or bar during the day, and a restaurant in the evening, this makes a pleasant day out from Pafos.

Grivas Boat
This is worth visiting if you are interested in recent Cypriot history. It lies half-way between Pafos and Coral Bay (ask the bus driver to let you off), beside the modern church of Agios Georgios. The Grivas Boat is an old caique, similar to the one in which the Cypriot-born Greek army colonel, George Grivas, landed, on this spot in 1954, to form EOKA and begin the guerrilla war against British rule.

Water sports All the sports facilities you could wish for are available at Coral Bay.

EXCURSIONS
Cape Drepano and Agios Georgios ★★★
Beside the fishing harbour here is a small beach and a view offshore to tiny Geronisos Island. The cliffs behind the beach are riddled with ancient rock cut tombs. At their summit stands the modern church of Agios Georgios and a far older chapel of the same name. The archaeological site at Agios Georgios church is worth a visit.
🕐 Open Mon–Sat 10.00–16.00, closed Sun ❶ Admission charge

RESORTS

Lara Bay ★★
About 5 km (3 miles) north of Cape Drepano is the Lara Bay Turtle Reserve, a protected beach where Cyprus's endangered green turtles lay their eggs.

RESTAURANTS
The approach road from Coral Bay to Pegeia is dotted with tavernas and the village centre is home to another cluster of eating places. All have similar menus, offer family cooking and a good atmosphere, and all are great value for money.

Coral Bay €€ This is the first restaurant on your left as you walk up the hill from Coral Beach into the Coral Bay resort. A wide selection of international and local dishes. Smart decor with indoor and outdoor seating. Also offers a traditional Sunday roast dinner! ⓐ Coral Bay Road ⓣ 26 62 17 90

Peyia Tavern €€ In the village centre, Peyia Tavern's owner tells you that *he* is the menu. Grilled meats are his speciality, accompanied by side dishes and washed down by village wine – you pay only for what you drink. ⓐ Pegeia village centre, near the church. ⓣ 26 62 10 77

Seriani €€ An attractive, informal restaurant surrounded by trees and plants, and serving a mix of Cypriot dishes, steaks and seafood. Fresh sea bream is the house speciality. Full English breakfast is also served. ⓐ Coral Bay Shopping Centre ⓣ 26 62 15 15

Vineyard €€ Set among scented fields outside the village, this taverna has both indoor and outdoor tables, and the home-cooked food is of a high standard. ⓐ Coral Bay Road ⓣ 26 62 21 71

◐ *The ancient chapel of Agios Georgios at Cape Drepano*

CORAL BAY & PEGEIA

RESORTS

Polis & Latsi (Latchi)
along the golden bay

Polis and Latsi are the haunts of 'alternative' tourists as well as being bases for exploring the rugged Akamas Peninsula and the scarcely developed north coast. The pace of life is slower here and there are far fewer discos and nightclubs than you find in bigger resorts.

THINGS TO SEE & DO
Boat trips ★★★
By taking a boat trip from Latsi harbour you can get a close-up view of the beautiful Akamas Peninsula without doing all the sweating that hikers do. You can take a 'barbecue boat', which goes along the coast and allows you to swim in the turquoise waters of the Blue Lagoon while your on-board barbecue is being prepared. There are also glass-bottomed boats, and you can hire your own power-boat to take you into tiny bays that no one else can reach.

Latsi ★★★
This is the main seaside resort on the north-western coast, and when you see how small Latsi is, it gives a good indication of the kind of tourism that rules in this area. The hotels are mostly small scale and the coast and interior are largely undeveloped – although there are clear signs that this happy state of affairs won't last for ever. Latsi is basically a fishing harbour, surrounded by a slew of excellent seafood restaurants and an adjacent beach. It is also the gateway to the Akamas Peninsula.

 The Polis tourist information office is at 2 Vasileos Stasioikou Street ❶ 26 32 24 68

Polis ★★★
A few kilometres east of Latsi, Polis is the main town in the area, and a place for shopping and dining out. The centre is attractive and maintains the intimate feel of this part of Cyprus. It stands at the heart

◆ *Seaside bar, Latsi*

of Chrysochou Bay and was the site of the ancient Greek port town of Marion, whose remains lie under the fields hereabouts. The town's main square, Dimarcheiou Plateia, and the surrounding streets form a mostly pedestrians-only zone, with a cluster of good restaurants with pavement terraces, café-bars where you can have a quick snack or a refreshing glass of fresh fruit juice, and shops selling newspapers, souvenirs and clothes.

Polis Archaeological Museum ★

Contains finds from the site of the ancient Greek city of Marion. It was destroyed in the wars of succession following the death of Alexander the Great, then later rebuilt and renamed Arsinoë. You can see a few of the remains amid orange groves. ⓐ Leoforos Archiepiskopou Makariou III, Polis, on the edge of town ⓘ 26 32 29 55 ⓘ Open Mon–Fri 08.00–14.00, Thurs 15.00–18.00, Sat 09.00–17.00 (Sept–June); Mon–Fri 08.00–14.00 and Sat 09.00–17.00 (July and August) ⓘ Admission charge

Water sports ★★★

As well as power-boat hire and diving with PADI instructors, the Latsi Water Sports Centre offers the chance to dive with the green turtles on a water-scooter in a group limited to four people. ⓐ Latsi main street ⓘ 26 32 20 95

RESORTS

RESTAURANTS

Archontariki €€ A traditional restaurant serving beautifully served Cypriot and international cuisine. There is also an outside eating garden. ⓐ 14 Leoforos Makarios ⓣ 26 32 13 28

Old Town €€ This is an attractive garden restaurant with the most extensive menu in Polis. The food is excellent and there are good vegetarian dishes. You can dine outside in the garden shaded by trellised vines. Prawns Santorini and sizzling steak are good choices. ⓐ Polis–Pafos Road ⓣ 26 32 27 58

Porto Latsi €€ A romantic, cellar-like interior makes a fine setting in which to eat the seafood served here – delivered fresh from the harbour across the road – but in fine weather the outside terrace beside the sea also has its fans. ⓐ Seafront, Latsi ⓣ 26 32 15 29

Yiangos and Peter €€–€€€ This friendly place would be one of the front-runners in any competition for Cyprus's best seafood restaurant. It has a great position beside Latsi harbour, and gets its fish straight off the boat. The fresh sea bream is excellent, as are the king prawns in garlic butter. ⓐ Latsi harbour ⓣ 26 32 14 11

Yiolou Tavern €€ Really good food at inexpensive prices. ⓐ Off the Pafos to Polis road ⓣ 26 63 30 20

BEACHES

The best and most accessible beaches are located at Latsi. Those along the north coast, towards Pomos, are usually deserted – partly because the sand is rough. The road from Latsi to the **Baths of Aphrodite** has many side-tracks that lead to the sea and small beaches of pebble and shingle. If you are willing to do some hiking, you will also find tiny deserted beaches on the Akamas Peninsula.

EXCURSIONS
Out & about

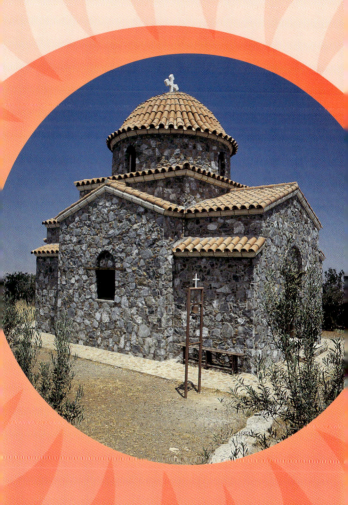

EXCURSIONS

Stavrovouni & Lefkara

The hills west of Larnaka rise up from the coastal plain through an increasingly rugged landscape, before merging with the eastern reaches of the Troodos Mountains in an area called Pitsilia.

Monasteries such as Stavrovouni find a natural home in this isolated country, and some of Cyprus's most unspoiled villages can be seen. One village, Lefkara, has earned an international reputation for its superb handmade lace.

Stavrovouni Monastery ★★

There used to be a shrine to Aphrodite on top of the 610 m/2000 ft high rocky outcrop where Stavrovouni now perches, with a view over a desolate landscape all the way to Lefkosia in one direction and to the sea in the other. St Helena, mother of the Roman Emperor Constantine the Great, founded the Mountain of the Cross Monastery in AD 327, endowing it with a piece of the True Cross she had picked up in the Holy Land. Ironically, today's women are allowed no closer than the car park.

Icon artistry Greek Orthodox religious icons that can cost up to several thousands pounds have been produced in the workshops at Stavrovouni Monastery for years. Father Kallinikos, renowned and admired throughout the area, has produced hundreds of icons in the old Byzantine way using tempera on linen over wood, or, more rarely, liquid wax and oils, sometimes mixed with 23-carat gold leaf. The icons, which are held in the highest regard by the Orthodox church, are still produced today.

Stavrovouni has been destroyed and rebuilt many times through the centuries, with its present incarnation dating from the 17th century. The venerated relic of the True Cross hangs beside the iconostasis (altar screen) in the church, covered in gold leaf and set in a silver-ornamented wooden crucifix. ❷ Off the Lefkosia–Lemesos road ❶ Open 08.00–noon and 15.00–18.00 (summer); 08.00–noon and 15.00–17.00 (winter) ❶ Admission free; men only; dress respectfully; no cameras

STAVROVOUNI & LEFKARA

 Renowned icon painter, Father Kallinikos

Lefkara ★★★

This is not one village but two – although Kato (Lower) Lefkara and Pano (Upper) Lefkara are only separated by a few hundred metres. Kato Lefkara's pastel-hued houses present a picture of idyllic charm, while Pano Lefkara is busier, with more shops, tavernas and parking places – but both of these pretty villages are worth visiting.

Lacemakers In both parts of Lefkara you will see women sitting out of doors, in good weather, painstakingly threading handmade Lefkara lace. Lace has been made in Lefkara for centuries, and Leonardo da Vinci is said to have visited Lefkara to buy lace for Milan Cathedral. Lefkaran men once travelled abroad for months at a time as sales representatives for these graceful products, leaving the women at home, stitching. Nowadays they do their selling from the village. Silverware and Turkish (or Cypriot) Delight, known as *loukoumi*, are other Lefkaran specialities.

EXCURSIONS

> **LACE CREATIONS**
> In *lefkaritika*, the traditional lacemaking style, no pattern is ever repeated. Mothers pass on their skills to their daughters, and visitors to Lefkara can watch three generations of the same family at work and see the beautiful patterns unfold: geometric motifs, a characteristic zigzag called 'the river' and natural patterns such as butterflies. Some pieces take as long as a year to make.

Royal Chapel of Agia Ekaterina ★

Some rough-road driving takes you across country on a dusty track from Lefkara via Klavia to Pyrga. Here an Orthodox monk is supervising what seems likely to be a decades-long renovation of the ruined medieval church of Agia Ekaterina. The church is notable not only for its isolated location and scenic outlook, but also for its own interest. 🕒 Open permanently ❶ Admission free

Agios Minas ★

Tucked into a little valley near Kato Drys, the flower-bedecked convent is a typically tranquil religious retreat. The nuns make and sell icons and honey, both of which are noted for their quality. 🕒 Open for group visits only, Mon to Fri ❶ Admission free; dress respectfully

Fikardou ★

This village, in the Troodos foothills, has a notable folk-architectural heritage. It has been declared a conservation zone to preserve the wooden-balconied houses dating from the Ottoman period, as well as the general rustic charm of this unspoiled Cypriot village.

Gourri ★

Not far from Fikardou, Gourri also has Ottoman-era houses with carved wooden balconies. Unlike its neighbour, however, it is not an official conservation zone.

STAVROVOUNI & LEFKARA

Machairas Monastery ★

The handsome monastic complex commands a magnificently scenic view over the rugged Pitsilia district. Machairas's history goes back to the 12th century, when an icon of the Virgin is said to have been found on the site, but today's structure dates from the early 20th century. The church has, however, hung on to its icon. An EOKA freedom fighter was killed near here by British troops in the 1950s, and his grave has become a place of pilgrimage for Cypriots. ❶ 22 35 93 34 ❷ Open for group visits only, Mon, Tues and Thurs 09.00–noon. ❸ Cameras and videos are not allowed. Admission free; dress respectfully

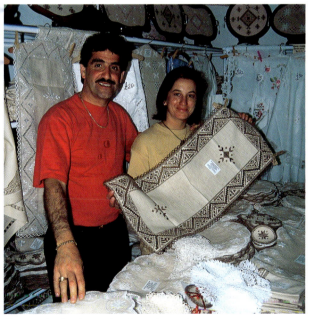

⬥ *Lace and embroidery work make good souvenirs*

CAPE KITI & AMATHOUS

Cape Kiti & Amathous
treasures of the coast

The coastline from Larnaka to Lemesos is relatively untouched by tourist development, except in the immediate neighbourhood of the two towns themselves.

Driving from one to the other on the coast road, or inland near the motorway, you will encounter several sites of interest that can be visited independently or on an organized tour.

Choirokoitia Neolithic Village ★★
In the foothills of the Troodos Mountains, the rough foundations of circular homes, which must have looked like big stone beehives, straggle up the steep slopes of a bleak promontory overlooking the Maroni River. They were occupied from the 7th to the 4th centuries BC by Stone Age people who buried their dead hunched up in the foetal position under the floors. They also made fertility symbols from conical stones.
✆ 24 322 710 ⏱ Open Mon–Fri 09.00–19.30, Sat–Sun 09.00–17.00 (summer); daily 09.00–17.00 (winter); daily 09.00–18.00 (spring and autumn) ❶ Admission charge

Kamares Aqueduct ★
South west of Larnaka, between the Lemesos road and the Salt Lake, are the 33 remaining arches of a ruined aqueduct built by the Ottoman Turks in the 18th century to bring water from the foothills of the Troodos to Larnaka.

Larnaka Salt Lake ★★
In winter, the lake bed here fills with shallow, salty water and pink flamingos are among the bird species that flock here to feed. By summer it has dried out to a hard, crystalline sheen and you can walk across it.

◐ *The ruined agora (marketplace) at Amathous*

EXCURSIONS

From a distance, the dried-up lake bed is a dazzling white. The salt used to be collected commercially but pollution from airliners using nearby Larnaka International Airport has made it unfit for human consumption. There is a Christian legend that Lazarus turned the soil to salt when a local woman refused to give him some grapes from her vineyard.

Hala Sultan Tekke ★★★

This mosque, set in a grove of palm trees on the shore of Larnaka Salt Lake, is famed for its tomb of Umm Haram, a relative of the Prophet Mohammed, who died here in AD 649 during an Arab raid on Cyprus. The stone that protects the sepulchre is covered in green cloths of mourning and is said to have flown miraculously from Mount Sinai in Egypt. Muslim ships sailing within sight of the shrine's domes and minarets used to lower their colours as a mark of respect. The mosque dates from the early 19th century, and the grandmother of the late King Hussein of Jordan is also entombed here (see also page 38). ⓛ Open daily 07.30–19.30 (summer); daily 07.30–17.00 (winter); daily 09.00–18.00 (spring and autumn)
ⓘ Admission free

Church of Panagia Angeloktisti ★★

At Kiti village, about 11 km (7 miles) west of Larnaka, Our Lady 'Built by the Angels' was rebuilt in the 11th century on a 5th-century foundation. The semi-circular apse is embellished with a 6th-century mosaic of the Virgin and Child accompanied by the Archangels Gabriel and Michael. One of only seven Byzantine religious mosaics to survive in the Orthodox world, the workmanship of its tiny squares of coloured and precious stones is outstanding, bearing comparison with those of the Byzantine Emperor Justinian and Empress Theodora in Ravenna's church of San Vitale in Italy. ⓛ Open 08.00–noon and 14.00–16.00 (until 18.00 July and August) ⓘ Admission free
ⓘ Visitors must dress respectfully

CAPE KITI & AMATHOUS

Kiti Tower ★
Beside the sea at rugged Cape Kiti, several kilometres from Kiti village, this is a stone watch-tower built by the Venetians as part of an early-warning system designed to prevent the invasion of Cyprus by the Turks in the 16th century. A lighthouse stands on steep cliffs close by the sea.

Zygi ★★
This is a small village on an undeveloped stretch of coastline. The day's catch from fishing harbours along the coast ends up on the menus of a line of good fish restaurants along the seafront.

Governor's Beach ★★
A popular beach east of Lemesos – its black sand soaks up the sun's heat. By noon it is scorching hot, so watch out for your bare feet!

Agios Georgios Alamanos Convent ★
The nuns here sell honey and icons at this tranquil convent near the coast, midway between Governor's Beach and Amathous. A nearby track leads to the sea at a rocky beach. ⏱ Open daily ❶ Admission free

Amathous ★★
Founded by the Phoenicians around 1000 BC, Amathous backed the Persians in the Greek wars, some 500 years later, but changed sides when Alexander the Great came knocking. Such pragmatism perhaps explains why so much survives – as much as England's King Richard the Lionheart saw when he landed at Amathous to attack Cyprus in 1191, on his way to the Crusades. There are the remains of the *acropolis* (hilltop fortress) and the *agora* (marketplace), as well as temples to Aphrodite, Adonis and Hercules. From the later era there are a Roman bath-house, an early Christian basilica and marble columns carved with a complex spiral pattern. The main archaeological site overlooks the sea 11 km (7 miles) east of Lemesos. ⏱ Open 09.00–19.30 (summer); 09.00–17.00 (winter); 09.00–18.00 (spring and autumn) ❶ Admission charge

EXCURSIONS

The Akrotiri Peninsula
soldiers and crusaders

Jutting into the Mediterranean west of Lemesos, the Akrotiri Peninsula is occupied almost entirely by the UK's Akrotiri Sovereign Base Area. Although much of the peninsula is accessible, the military installations around RAF Akrotiri are closed to the public, putting the promontories at Cape Zevgari and Cape Gata out of bounds. Only small-scale commercial activity is allowed, which has preserved the peninsula's natural environment from over-development.

THE AKROTIRI PENINSULA

Kolossi Castle ★★★
About 14 km (8.5 miles) west of Lemesos, Kolossi Castle was the Grand Commandery of the Knights of the Order of St John of Jerusalem, and later of the Knights Templar, after the Crusaders were driven out of the Holy Land in 1291. The existing structure dates from 1454. A romantic lookout place, with stout walls and turreted battlements, Kolossi withstood sieges by Genoese and Mameluke invaders. In addition to the central keep, there are the remains of a basilica, a sugar factory and an aqueduct. Fleur-de-lys symbols are carved on walls and fireplaces, and the entrance hall of the keep has a mural of the crucifixion.
❶ 25 93 49 07 ❷ Open daily 09.00–19.30 (summer); daily 09.00–17.00 (winter); daily 09.00–18.00 (spring and autumn) ❸ Admission charge

Kourion Archaeological Museum ★
Finds from excavations at the nearby archaeological sites of Kourion and the Sanctuary of Apollo Ylatis (see page 79) are displayed here, including pottery, oil-lamps, coins, ornaments, *amphorae* (wine- and oil-storage jars), sculptures and votive offerings. A poignant group of three skeletons – almost certainly a husband, wife and their small child – huddle together as fate left them when they perished in the earthquake that demolished Kourion in AD 365. ❶ 25 93 24 53 ❷ Open Mon–Fri 09.00–14.30, and Thurs 15.00–17.00 (except in Aug), closed Sat and Sun ❸ Admission charge

Episkopi Barracks ★
The Royal Air Force base at Akrotiri is one of the UK's two Sovereign Base Areas in Cyprus (the other is at Dhekelia, near Larnaka). A little piece of Britain beside the Mediterranean, the SBA's Episkopi Barracks is modelled on an English suburb. Inside, the military personnel and their families have their own houses, shops, churches, banks, hospitals and sports facilities such as cricket fields and polo pitches. The coast road from Lemesos to Pafos runs through the barracks.

◐ *A small boy explores an archaeological site at Kourion*

EXCURSIONS

Akrotiri Salt Lake ★★

Although dried out in summer, the lake is filled with shallow water in winter and is a great place for bird-watchers. You can see pink flamingos, ducks, waders and other species, including the Cyprus warbler, black-winged stilt, chukar, crested lark, marsh sandpiper, broad-billed sandpiper, egret, heron and little ringed plover. The flamingos feed on small crustaceans that flourish in the salty water. In summer, the glittering salt lake looks as if it has a solid surface, but do not try to cross it on foot, by bike or in a vehicle – it isn't as hard as it looks.

Agios Nikolaos ton Gaton ★

The monastery of St Nicholas of the Cats is so called because of the cats supposedly introduced to Cyprus in the 4th century by St Helena, the mother of the Roman Emperor, Constantine the Great, to rid the island of poisonous snakes. There are still plenty of cats at Agios Nikolaos, basking in the glow of their forefathers' victory, watched over by the nuns. The original monastery was founded during Constantine's reign (AD 324–37) but the present structure comprises the restored remnants of a 13th-century abbey abandoned when the Ottoman Turks invaded Cyprus in 1570. ◐ Open daily ❶ Admission free

Lady's Mile Beach ★★

This long, sandy and – usually – deserted stretch of beach lies just outside Lemesos and is named after the place where the wife of a British officer walked her horse during the colonial period. Frequent strong winds make the waters here an excellent arena for windsurfing. Its major drawback is the unsightly view across to the harbour installations at Lemesos.

Fassouri plantations ★

A green area of citrus groves has been established around the village of Fassouri, west of Lemesos. You can drive or cycle around the orchards on roads shaded from the sun by cypress trees, while breathing in air scented with the tang of oranges, lemons and grapefruit.

● *Kolossi Castle*

Boat trip ★★

A trip around Akrotiri Peninsula can be made by excursion boat from Lemesos. Leaving the fishing harbour, you pass the busy commercial port, with its constant stream of cargo ships coming and going. From there you cruise past sandy Lady's Mile Beach on the eastern shore of the peninsula, with the Salt Lake visible behind. RAF Akrotiri lies out of sight behind a screen of sand dunes and vegetation.

Rounding Cape Gata, then Cape Zevgari, you sail along the western shore, then get a spectacular view of the cliffside at Kourion, on which the ruins of the ancient city stand. Pissouri Bay makes a fine place to come close inshore for a swim. The tour ends with a close-up view of the Rock of Aphrodite. There are frequent excursions from Lemesos fishing harbour.

EXCURSIONS

Kourion
and the Sanctuary of Apollo Ylatis: glories of antiquity

Spend a few hours in the world of the ancient Greeks and Romans at the dramatic clifftop city of Kourion, overlooking the sea, and further along the coast, at the well-preserved Sanctuary of Apollo Ylatis. When you add in famous historic sites and the attractive seaside resort of Pissouri beach, the experience combines into a memorable day out.

Kourion (Curium) ★★★

The ruins of the ancient city are perched on a clifftop overlooking the sea 19 km (12 miles) west of Lemesos. Kourion was founded by Greek colonists in the 14th century BC. It was an important city-state throughout Cyprus's early history, and reached its peak of influence under the Romans. It was destroyed by an earthquake in AD 365, rebuilt and finally abandoned after Arab raids in the 7th century. ❶ 25 99 10 48 ❷ Open daily 08.00–19.30 (summer); daily 08.00–17.00 (winter); daily 08.00–18.00 (spring and autumn) ❸ Admission charge

Theatre and mosaics ★★

There are three main parts to the site. The first includes the Odeon, a magnificent Greco-Roman theatre, built into the cliff face and with a stunning view. Visitors pose theatrically for snapshots on the stage, one of the great sites of the ancient world. Beside it is the House of Eustolios, a private Roman villa dating from the 4th century AD. One of its mosaics shows a young woman, who symbolizes the Creation.

In the second part of the site is an early Christian basilica, a 5th-century church overlooking the sea. The nearby Roman forum is still being excavated. In this zone is a Roman water reservoir that seems to have been Kourion's main water distribution centre. A residential area flanking the forum has a number of buildings containing fine mosaics, including those in the House of the Gladiators and the House of Achilles.

KOURION

Located 2 km (1 mile) west of the main site, the city's stadium, dated to the 2nd century AD, was an arena for track and field sports. Not much remains, apart from the lower reaches of its wall.
🕐 Open permanently
ℹ Admission included in entry price from main site

Kourion Drama Festival ★
In summer, the Odeon at Kourion features performances of plays by ancient Greek writers, Shakespeare and modern dramatists, as well as classical and modern music, ballet performances and sound-and-light shows. Check with the tourist office for programme details.

🔺 *Sanctuary of Apollo Ylatis*

Sanctuary of Apollo Ylatis ★★

About 3 km (2 miles) west of Kourion are the remains of the Sanctuary of Apollo Ylatis, an important temple and place of pilgrimage in ancient times. Dormitories and halls can be clearly seen, along with an exercise court, a baths complex and the Priest of Apollo's house.

At the heart of the sanctuary is the partially restored Temple of Apollo. Any visitors sacrilegious enough to touch the altar of Apollo were thrown into the sea from the nearest headland – so be careful!
📞 25 99 10 49 🕐 Open daily 09.00–19.30 (summer); daily 09.00–17.00 (winter); daily 09.00–18.00 (spring and autumn) ℹ Admission charge

EXCURSIONS

Pissouri & Kouklia
sea foam and sea-born Aphrodite

The wild and scenic coastline – stretching from the ancient city of Kourion to the Rock of Aphrodite about midway between Lemesos and Pafos – is worth seeing just for its own beauty.

Kouklia ★
This village is the site of Palaia Pafos, sometimes known as Palea Paos meaning Old Pafos, one of ancient Cyprus's most important city states. On a hill outside Kouklia, archaeologists have excavated part of the city walls, uncovering a siege mound and counter-tunnels dating from the Cypriot rebellion against Persia in 498 BC. Despite indications of fierce resistance, the rebel city was eventually captured.

Sanctuary of Aphrodite ★
Although its ruins are now sparse and hard to interpret, this shrine to the Greek goddess of love was once renowned throughout the ancient Mediterranean. It was said that all Cypriot women were obliged to 'offer' themselves to the 'pilgrims' who came here in colourful processions.

Holes dug in the walls seem to have been made by robbers looking for hidden treasure. The on-site museum is housed in an Ottoman-era farm, called the Chiftlik, and displays finds from the Sanctuary, including a conical stone that may have been an archaic cult idol of Aphrodite.
ⓐ Kouklia village ❶ 26 43 21 80 ❶ Open daily 09.00–16.00
❶ Admission charge

Rock of Aphrodite (Petra tou Romiou) ★★★
This unusual rock formation, standing in shallow sea water beside the Lemesos–Pafos road, must be the most famous spot in Cyprus. This is where Aphrodite, goddess of beauty and love, was born, wafted ashore on a seashell, to be met by her handmaidens, the Hours, who decked her out with precious jewels, set a crown of gold on her head, and gave her

▲ *Pissouri Bay*

> **UNKINDEST CUT**
> According to the ancient Greek writer Hesiod, the white foam from which Aphrodite arose came from the genitals of Uranos, which had been severed by his son Kronos and cast into the sea. In reality – if the term can be applied to mythology – she was possibly imported from the Near East as a fertility goddess.

earrings of gold and copper. Aphrodite's Rock is a favourite spot for romantic couples, particularly at sunset. ❸ The beach is reached via a tunnel under the busy coast road from the Cyprus Tourism Organisation car park and rest area 🕒 Open permanently ❗ Admission free

Pissouri Beach ★★★

Reached via a side-road off the Lemesos–Pafos road, Pissouri's beach is lined with tavernas where the local wine can be tried. There is also an anchorage in the harbour where fishing and small cruise boats moor.

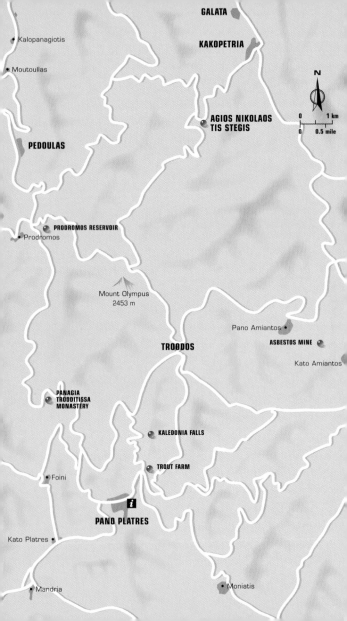

THE TROODOS MOUNTAINS

The Troodos Mountains
citadel of tranquillity

In summer the cool air of the Troodos Mountains, scented with eucalyptus and pine, is an irresistible draw for many otherwise beachbound tourists. There are nature reserves and forest stations to explore, as well as Byzantine-era monasteries.

ROUTE
Pafos and Lemesos are the resorts closest to the Troodos Mountains. This day-trip itinerary begins in Pafos, snakes its way through many of the mountains' stellar sights, then rolls downhill to end in Lemesos. You can easily do the route in reverse, beginning in Lemesos and ending in Pafos. In either case, you return to your home base on the A1 motorway, which now runs from Lemesos to Pafos.

Take the Lemesos road from Pafos, through Geroskipou and past Pafos Airport, to Kouklia, where you turn left, passing the big Asprokremmos Dam. At Nikokleia village, you have a choice; you can either take the lower road, to the right, along the Diarizos river valley, or the higher road, to the left, which follows the ridgeline for part of the way, looking down into the neighbouring valley of the Xeros Potamos river. Both ways are scenic, and both bring you out near Filousa village, where you follow signs for Agios Nikolaos tis Stegis and Pano Platres, for a refreshment break.

Pano Platres
The main mountain resort, Pano Platres, and its neighbouring Kato Platres are as popular in summer as they are during the winter skiing season. The Troodos Mountains tourist office is here, in Village Square, providing maps and booklets on signposted mountain trails ⓘ 25 42 13 16. Tumbling 18 m (60 ft), Kaledonia Falls near Plano Platres are fed by a perennial stream, the Kryos.

The mile-long Kaledonia Trail follows a route through the forest to the falls from near Troodos village. Continue uphill through Pano Platres,

EXCURSIONS

passing a trout farm and the pathway to Kaledonia Falls outside town. Follow the winding road up through the mountains to Troodos – the President of Cyprus's summer residence is somewhere off to your right, out of sight among the trees.

Troodos

Troodos village, near the roof of the mountains, has gift shops, tavernas and car parks, and makes a bustling change from the loneliness of the mountain trails. Go right at the crossroads in Troodos, passing the disused asbestos mine at Pano Amiantos and the desolate scenery it has left on the mountainside, and descend the northern slopes of the mountains, towards Kakopetria.

Kakopetria

Kakopetria is a fast-growing resort on the northern edge of the mountains but close enough to make a convenient base for exploring them. Its old village centre is being preserved. The **Maryland at the Mill restaurant** here (see page 87) is a tall, wood-built place, overlooking a mountain stream. Continue downhill a short way, to Galata.

Galata

Galata is a handsome village of white-painted houses at the head of the fertile Solea Valley. It has a small **Folk Art Museum** and a restored Ottoman inn. Two old churches just outside the village are on UNESCO's list of World Cultural Heritage Sites for their superb religious frescos: **Panagia Podythou Church**, and the nearby timber-roofed church of **Archangelos Michail and Panagia Theotokos**. Return to Galata, and make a short detour to the right, to Agios Nikolaos tis Stegis.

Agios Nikolaos tis Stegis

This 11th-century Byzantine church with two roofs, the outer being a protection against snow, is a UNESCO World Cultural Heritage Site, thanks to an interior which is decorated with religious frescos.

◬ *Troodos Square in winter*

Its scenic location probably has as much to do with attracting visitors, however. You now have to return to Troodos, and turn right at the village crossroads, to Mount Olympus.

Mount Olympus

The Troodos Mountains rise up to the peak of Mount Olympus, which is 1952 m (nearly 6500 ft) high. In winter you can ski the snows of Olympus and in summer hike its nature trails. The summit is occupied by the dome of a British military radar station. Continue down the north-western face of the mountains, past Prodromos Reservoir, to Prodromos.

Prodromos

This is the location of the Cyprus Forestry College, whose graduates play a big part in the effort to restore the island's tree cover. Prodromos stands at an altitude of 1390 m (4560 ft), and has a fine view of villages further down the slopes, ironically because it is in an area that has not been heavily forested. Continue downhill to Pedoulas.

Pedoulas

This village in the Marathasa Valley is famous for its cherries. In June, roadside stalls are filled with the dark fruit, piled up in baskets like heaps

EXCURSIONS

of precious stones. One of the Troodos Mountains' most popular resorts, Pedoulas has several good restaurants. The village's **Ecclesiastical Museum** ❶ 22 95 36 36, and Archangelos Michail Church, are worth a visit. Continue downhill to Moutoullas.

Moutoullas

This is an attractive Marathasa Valley village, whose 13th-century Byzantine church of Panagia tou Moutoullas is aother UNESCO World Cultural Heritage Site. Continue downhill to Kalopanagiotis.

Kalopanagiotis

Formerly a spa resort thanks to its sulphur springs, nowadays visitors come to see the three side-by-side churches, under a single snow roof, of Agios Ioannis Lampadistis Monastery, a UNESCO World Cultural Heritage Site. Return to Prodromos and take the lower road to Pano Platres, passing Panagia Trooditissa Monastery.

Panagia Trooditissa Monastery

Overlooking a steep gorge some 5 km (3 miles) from Pano Platres, rustic Trooditissa (🕒 Open daily ❶ Admission free), founded in the 13th century, boasts a priceless silver-gilt icon of the Madonna. Continue to a side road leading off to the right to Foini village.

Foini

A pretty little village with steep streets, clinging to the hillside, Foini is noted for its traditional Cypriot pottery as well as modern ware, and its Folk Art Museum. Take the road through Kato Platres, which puts you on the road to Lemesos.

 If you are fit and feeling slightly adventurous, a wonderful way to see the mountains is from the saddle of a mountain bike, for hire in Plano Platres and Kakopetria.

THE TROODOS MOUNTAINS

● *A village in the Troodos Mountains*

RESTAURANTS

Civic € A restaurant popular with locals, which offers tourists the chance to sample traditional Cypriot dishes. Seating inside and out. International dishes also available. ⓐ Located in Paliometocho village between Troodos and Lefkosia ⓘ 22 83 56 40

Maryland at the Mill €€ A popular, high-sited restaurant noted for its excellent mountain trout, and with a full Cypriot and international menu. ⓐ Village centre, Kakopetria ⓘ 22 92 25 36

EXCURSIONS

Troodos wine villages
glistening grapes and golden days

Spread across the southern and western foothills of the Troodos Mountains are the vineyards from which Cypriot wines are derived. The vineyards remain the key to prosperity and continued existence for many villages here, where life moves at its own pace and rhythm, and thousands of families are involved in grape production. Wine is among Cyprus's most important exports, with Britain its main customer.

Commandaria region
A narrow slice of the southern Troodos wine district is given over to the production of the grapes used to make the distinctive Commandaria dessert wine. Dotted with villas and pretty villages, the region has an ambience similar to European wine-producing regions such as Tuscany.

Krassochoria
Off the south-western edge of the Troodos Mountains is another grape-growing region, the Krassochoria (Wine Villages), whose villagers are up to their knees in grape juice come autumn – or at any rate, they would be, if the whole process hadn't by now been automated.

THE ROUTE
Beginning and ending in Lemesos, this route leads you through the heart of the district, with spectacular scenery and mountain villages. Leave Lemesos on the A1 motorway east, until junction 21, where you turn off towards Parekklisia. Follow this road north through Kellaki, turn left at Eptagoneia to Arakapas, then right through Sykopetra to Palaichori.

Palaichori
The Byzantine-era village, with its white-painted houses and red-tiled roofs, looks like an avalanche frozen in the act of tumbling down the

▶ *Grape harvesting*

TROODOS WINE VILLAGES

EXCURSIONS

steep hillside to which it clings. Vineyards (with grapes that produce a fine red wine), orchards, almond trees and vegetable patches form a delightful pastoral background. Leave Palaichori on the Agios Theodoros road and turn right following the signs for Agros.

Agros

A pretty village that produces rose-water, mineral water and wine (not necessarily in that order of preference) as liquid inducements to make a visit. Leave Agros to the south, on the road through Kato Mylos to Zoopyi.

Zoopyi

One of the villages that produces the Commandaria dessert wine, Zoopyi is surrounded by vineyards in a beautifully green area off the southern slopes of the Troodos. It is also an important producer of *zivania* (also called 'Cyprus whisky'), distilled from the skin, pips and other grape bits left over after the wine has been fermented. The alcohol is so strong that Cypriots wisely drink it in moderation.

From Zoopyi continue south a short way, to a crossroads and turn right (west), through Agios Mamas, to Pera Pedi, where you go south a short distance to Koilani.

Koilani

A village in the heart of the grape-growing, wine-making district of the southern Troodos, Koilani keeps one foot in heaven's camp with its Ecclesiastical Museum. Housed within the grounds of the village church, the museum's collection includes icons, religious vessels, antique prayer books and ornaments, some of which display fine craftsmanship in silver. Return to Pera Pedi and continue west to Mandria, where you turn south towards Omodos.

Omodos

The largest of the Krassochoria wine villages, Omodos has acted to preserve its traditional character while benefiting from tourism. The village centre has been restored, arts and crafts workshops have been

TROODOS WINE VILLAGES

established, and some residents invite visitors for a guided tour of their traditional homes. In addition, there is a restored 15th-century wine press known as *linos*. A wine festival is held in the village every August.

Among the goods for sale are the local lace, called *pipilla*, and ring-shaped bread, called *arketana*. The restored house interiors are hung with gourds, and kitchen utensils hang beside the traditional wood-fired oven. The houses also have cellars where large earthenware pots, called *pitharia*, formerly filled with wine, are kept.

The Monastery of Stavros, in Omodos, has a golden cross containing hemp fibres said to have come from the ropes which bound Jesus to the Cross, and another that is said to contain a fragment of the True Cross. Continue south on the main road, making a short detour outside of town to Vasa.

Vasa

Wine and mineral water are produced and bottled in this red-roofed Krassochoria village near Omodos. Vasa is also renowned for its mineral water, bottled here from the village spring. The house of the noted Cypriot poet Lipertis, who died in 1937, has been restored and can be visited. Return to the main road and continue south to Agios Amvrosios.

Agios Amvrosios

'Green' wines are produced from organically grown grapes in this southern Troodos village, at the **Ecological Winery** (25 24 39 81 Open Mon–Fri 08.00–14.00) owned by Georgios Yiallouros. The winery produces up to 60,000 bottles of environmentally sound wines a year, which taste quite good. Stay on the main road south, back to Lemesos.

A BITE TO EAT
There are several cafés around the main square in Omodos, but for traditional Cypriot cooking, try the **Ambelothea Restaurant** €€ Near the hospital 25 42 13 66

EXCURSIONS

Cruising to Egypt & the Greek Islands

A holiday in Cyprus puts you in easy reach of the wonders of Egypt and the beautiful Greek Islands. The best way to take advantage of this is to enjoy one of the many cruises on offer departing from Lemesos. There are a number of cruise and tour options available.

Getting there
Several companies operate cruises from Cyprus to Egypt and the Greek Islands. Cruises can be booked easily through your holiday representative or the tourist office as well as direct with the cruise lines. Full information is also readily available from:

- **Louis Cruise Lines** ☏ 25 57 00 00 🆎 25 57 33 20
  Ⓦ www.louiscruises.com
- **Salamis Tours** ☏ 25 86 06 00 🆎 25 36 19 81
  Ⓦ www.salamis-tours.com

While many of the cruises on offer follow similar itineraries, circumstances may cause changes to be introduced at short notice. The descriptions below give some details about what is on offer, but should not be considered as an exact description of the itinerary.

Three-night cruise to Egypt
Depart Lemesos and arrive in Port Said, located at the entrance of the Suez Canal, at around 06.00 hours. After breakfast onboard, you disembark and are taken by air-conditioned coach to the ruins of the historic City of Memphis, once the capital of Ancient Egypt.

After leaving Memphis, you will visit a Papyrus Institute to see the oldest type of paper in the world being made, and then you'll be taken to see the Great Pyramids at Giza. The burial chambers of the Egyptian Pharaohs are located surprisingly close to Cairo and offer a wonderful opportunity to view the past – especially the Great Pyramid of Khufu,

CRUISING TO EGYPT & THE GREEK ISLANDS

The Great Pyramids at Giza

one of the Seven Wonders of the World, which stands alongside those of Khafre and Menkaure at the Giza Plateau. The visit will also give you the option to see inside the third Pyramid and/or visit the Sun Boat which was constructed to take the Pharaoh on journeys in the afterlife. From here you will continue to visit the mysterious Sphinx and its Temple before returning to the ship for the night.

The next day you will visit Cairo – the heart of ancient Egyptian civilization, and one of the most fascinating cities in the world. First stop is a visit to the Egyptian Museum, where some of the world's most stunning pieces of antiquity can be found. Some of the most precious items ever found can be admired here, including the treasures from the tomb of Tutankhamen and an extensive collection of jewellery.

EXCURSIONS

After the Museum, you will visit the oldest church in Cairo, the Hanging Church, which contains relics from the early days of Christianity in Egypt. From here, you will be driven to the Citadel of Salah El Din, which houses the world-famous Alabaster Mosque. From high up on the walls of the Citadel, you can enjoy a panoramic view of Cairo.

After leaving Cairo, you will be returned to Port Said where, after embarkation, the ship sails for Lemesos.

Numerous other options are also available for cruises to the region, including trips to Alexandria and Beirut. Please contact one of the cruise lines mentioned above for further details.

Greek Islands

Select a cruise to the stunning Greek Islands and leave Lemesos for a fascinating voyage exploring the wonders of the Mediterranean.

Highlights of the Greek Islands include the Lindos area of Rhodes, which was established around 3000 years ago and was one of the most important civilizations of the Ancient World. Visit the Temple of Lindian Athena, built in 550 BC and rebuilt in the 3rd century BC in the form that you see it today. St Paul was shipwrecked at Lindos and founded the Rhodia Church, and the bay next to Lindos Acropolis is still known as St Paul's Bay. The island was also occupied by the Knights of St John, who fortified the Acropolis to protect it against invasion from the Saracens. The old Byzantine church dedicated to the Holy Mother can still be seen inside the Acropolis.

On the island of Kos, visit the Asklipieon, which was built in the 4th century BC and dedicated to Hippocrates, Father of Modern Medicine. Due to the sloping terrain, the Sanctuary is constructed on three terraces and joined by a magnificent staircase. The first level, the Courtyard of the Temple, was used for various ceremonies and festivals, while the second level is the Great Altar of the Temple. The third level is the Doric Temple of Asklipius, dating from the 2nd century.

A number of cruises are available to the Greek Islands. Please check with the tour operators for destinations, itineraries and prices either before you leave, or once you arrive in Cyprus.

LIFESTYLE
Island life

LIFESTYLE

Food & drink

Cypriots are rarely happier than when piling convivially into the heaped-up contents of as many food platters as will set a table groaning, but not quite collapsing. You should join them as often as possible, eating out at least several times a week at a traditional taverna. Don't lock yourself up in the hotel restaurant eating 'international' food. Get out, trust your nose, and follow wherever it leads.

CYPRIOT FOOD

Your best guide, if you want to taste the genuine flavour of Cypriot food, is to see where the locals go, and go with them. Eating out in Cyprus is a social event and traditional Cypriot cuisine lends itself to the experience. *Meze* is the best introduction – a torrent of little dishes that arrive on the table in a seemingly endless flood.

Cyprus stands at the crossroads of three continents (Africa, Europe and Asia), and it has absorbed culinary influences from all three. Ordering a *meze* enables you to sample the results in the form of some 20 to 30 dishes, ranging from dips and raw vegetables to fish and meat in richly flavoured sauces. Such a meal is a test of appetite and endurance, another reason why Cypriots linger so long over their meals.

Among many *meze* items are: *haloumi* – a cheese made from the milk of thyme-fed goats, often served grilled; *dolmadakia* – vine leaves stuffed with rice and meat; *lountza* – smoked pork, marinaded in red wine; *tahini* – a sesame-seed dip mixed with lemon, garlic and parsley; and *houmous* – a dip made from chickpeas and olive oil.

Main dishes include such favourites as *afelia* – chunks of pork stewed in a red-wine sauce sprinkled with coriander; *souvlakia* – lamb or pork grilled on a skewer; *keftedes* – fried meatballs; *moussaka* – a layered dish of aubergines, potato and minced meat in a béchamel sauce; and *kleftiko* – lamb roasted in an earthenware oven.

● *Ordering a meze is a good way to sample the local food*

LIFESTYLE

LIFESTYLE

BRITISH
As the British make up the single biggest group of foreign visitors to Cyprus, no major resort is without its line-up of traditional British favourites: fish and chips, mushy peas, black pudding, roast beef and the full English breakfast. Pub grub has its place too. As in Britain, you can also find a more considered interpretation of British cuisine, with fresh ingredients, home baking, regional specialities and vegetarian food.

INTERNATIONAL
Among the German restaurants and bars serving *currywurst* (curry sausage), grilled meats and marvellous German beers, and the Scandinavian restaurants, with their *smorgasbords* and smoked salmon, you will also find Russian restaurants catering for the large number of Russian visitors. Italian and Mexican-style restaurants are popular, as is American-inspired fast food, including McDonald's and Pizza Hut.

WINE
Cypriot wines run the gamut from light and sparkling to full-bodied red, with most popular attention being focused on the light and fruity whites. Commandaria, a sweet red dessert wine with a history dating back to ancient times, is one of Cyprus's most notable products.

Good yet inexpensive wines are plentiful. The Ecological Winery at Agios Amvrosios produces wines from organically grown grapes. Panagia Chrysorrogiatissa monastery, near Pano Panagia, has won respect for its high-quality Monte Royia wines. In a taverna, you can't go far wrong if you ask for either the red or white house wine – it will usually have come from some small village vineyard and will be perfectly acceptable.

Other drinks
Carlsberg has a brewery in Cyprus, and the local KEO and LEON lagers are every bit as good. English beers are a 'speciality' of British pubs on the island. In some bars you will find international beers as well. Cypriot brandy is cheaper and lighter than the French version, and is the main ingredient of 'Brandy Sour', Cyprus's own cocktail.

LIFESTYLE

Cyprus produces many fine local wines

THE KAFENEION

In many Greek villages, the *kafeneion* (café) remains very much a male preserve, although visitors of both sexes will be made welcome. Customers come here to read the paper, debate the issues of the day and play backgammon, as well as to consume café *hellenico* (Greek coffee). This is made by boiling finely ground coffee beans in a special pot with a long handle. Sugar is added during the preparation rather than at the table, so be sure to order it *glyko* (sweet), *metrio* (medium) or *sketo* (no sugar). In the summer, try *frappé* (with ice) to cool down.

LIFESTYLE

Menu decoder

Here are some of the authentically Greek dishes that you might encounter in tavernas or pastry shops.

baklava A sweet pastry popular throughout the Middle East made with finely chopped nuts, honey and filo pastry

dolmadákia Vine leaves stuffed with rice, onions, dill, parsley, mint and lemon juice

domátes/piperiés yemistés Tomatoes/peppers stuffed with herb-flavoured rice (and sometimes minced lamb or beef)

fasólia saláta White beans (haricot, butter beans) dressed with olive oil, lemon juice, parsley, onions, olives and tomato

horiátiki saláta Country salad (known in England as 'Greek salad'); every restaurant in Cyprus has its own recipe, but the basic ingredients usually consist of tomatoes, cucumber, onions, green peppers, black olives, oregano and feta cheese, dressed with vinegar, olive oil and oregano

kadaifi A sweet pastry with shredded wheat, nuts and honey syrup

lazánia sto fourno Greek lasagne, similar to Italian lasagne, but often including additional ingredients, such as chopped boiled egg or sliced Greek-style sausages

makaronópitta A pie made from macaroni blended with beaten eggs, cheese and milk, baked in puff pastry

melitzanópitta Vegetarian pie made from baked and then liquidized aubergines mixed with onions, garlic, breadcrumbs, eggs, mint and parmesan cheese

melitzanosalátta Dip made from baked aubergines, liquidized with tomatoes, onions and lemon juice

moussakás Moussaka, made from fried slices of aubergines, interlayered with minced beef and béchamel sauce

pítta me kymá Meat pie made from minced lamb and eggs, flavoured with onions and cinnamon and baked in filo pastry

LIFESTYLE

 ▲ *The best place to buy fresh produce, the local market*

pastíccio Layers of macaroni, *haloumi* cheese and minced meat (cooked with onions, tomatoes and basil), topped with béchamel sauce and baked
souvlákia Kebab – usually of pork cooked over charcoal
spanakopítta Cigar-shaped pies made from feta cheese, eggs, spinach, onions and nutmeg in filo pastry
taramosaláta Cod's roe dip made from puréed potatoes, smoked cod's roe, oil, lemon juice and onion
tyropitákia Small triangular cheese pies made from feta cheese and eggs in filo pastry
tzatzíki Grated cucumber and garlic in a dressing of yoghurt, olive oil and vinegar

LIFESTYLE

Shopping

CYPRUS HANDICRAFT SERVICE
The government-operated Cyprus Handicraft Service (CHS) is a key part of the drive to retain the island's traditional arts and crafts. All of these are under serious threat as children no longer learn the old skills from their parents, and the villages which were the source of many traditional practices are abandoned in favour of the modern towns and resorts. CHS operates a centre in Lefkosia that provides teaching and practical experience, and it has shops in Lefkosia, Larnaka, Lemesos and Pafos. It produces a limited range of well-made items in all kinds of traditional crafts – pottery, embroidery, woodwork, metalwork, and so on (see page 22).

ICONS
Greek Orthodox religious icons are painted and sold at many monasteries and convents, and local priests may also try their hand. Most are simple items, but others are superb pieces of art in demand around the world. Among the latter are those produced at Stavrovouni Monastery, which can cost up to several thousand pounds each (see page 66).

LACE
Lace has been made in Lefkara for centuries in the traditional style called *lefkaritika*, each piece being a unique creation of the village women who sit outdoors in good weather, hand-stitching intricate designs on to pieces of Irish linen. The lace can most easily be bought in Lefkara itself, with the added attraction of seeing how it is made, but it can also be bought at shops and markets elsewhere (see page 67).

LOOM EMBROIDERY
There are several traditional styles of woven cloth. Pafos is noted for *paphitika*, bright geometric designs woven into cloths, cushion-covers, bedspreads, curtains, tablecloths and other domestic items. Then there are *lefkonika* – towels, aprons and place-mats – and *alatjia*,

Traditional loom embroidery is popular with locals and tourists alike

a silky-smooth striped cotton. Silk takes the limelight at Geroskipou village, near Pafos, which is noted for this material.

POTTERY

The resurgence of craft work in pottery and ceramics means that some sophisticated jugs, bowls and other objects are now being produced. You can find these in good souvenir shops, as well as in market areas of the main towns. One of the best craft potters is the **Lemba Pottery** (❶ 26 27 08 22), at Lemba village near Pafos.

Traditional pottery is also made at Koloni, Foini (Phini) and Geroskipou. Huge hand thrown *pitharia* pots, from Kornos, were once used for storing olive oil and wine. They can still be seen, but are now more likely to be filled with flowers. Lapithos village, in what is now the Turkish-occupied part of Cyprus, became known for its porcelain cats, a tradition that was popularized by the British in pre-independence days. Nowadays, Lapithos cats are produced in the South.

LIFESTYLE

Kids

AGIA NAPA
This resort is well supplied with facilities for keeping demanding little consumers amused. There are kamikaze slides, river tube rides and rolling logs at Water World Water Park (page 29), while at EMW Go-Karts (page 28) kids can test their skill and nerves (and no doubt their parents' nerves as well) on a junior racing circuit. Dinosaur Park (page 28) has models of prehistoric creatures, complete with sounds. The Municipal Museum of Marine Life is a new museum showcasing the wide variety of marine life around Cyprus's coast (page 28).

AKAMAS PENINSULA
Monk seals can be seen off the Akamas Peninsula (page 62) and some 168 bird species and 55 butterfly species have been identified on it, as well as 600 or more plant varieties, so it could be good for a 'nature studies' walk. The nearby waters of the Baths of Aphrodite are said to confer eternal youth, something which might seem more desirable to adults than to children.

AKROTIRI PENINSULA
The Salt Lake (page 76) dries out to a muddy salt flat in summer and in winter its shallow waters are visited by pink flamingos. Nearby Kolossi Castle (page 75) was once the base of the Knights Templar, so it's a great place for pretending to be a gallant knight or a distressed maiden.

LEMESOS
How about making black sandcastles? Governor's Beach (page 73), east of Lemesos, has the black sand you need as a raw material. Lemesos's small Zoo is in the Municipal Gardens.

◐ *Enjoy the ride at Water World Water Park*

LIFESTYLE

Sports & activities

GOLF

Cyprus is not a noted golfing destination, but it is trying to remedy that situation and now has three good golf courses in the Pafos area. Combined with sunshine they certainly make a worthwhile outing for golfers.

- **Tsada Golf Club** – 18 holes, par 72 ❶ 26 64 27 74
- **Secret Valley Golf Club** – 18 holes, par 71 ❶ 26 64 27 74
- **Aphrodite Hills Golf and Leisure Centre** – 18 holes, par 71
  ❶ 26 81 87 00

LIFESTYLE

HIKING

There are many hiking and nature trails in Cyprus. Serious hikers will want to plan their own routes into the Troodos Mountains, the Akamas Peninsula, or rugged areas around the resorts. Even if all you want to do is a little energetic walking while getting close to nature, but without the paraphernalia of maps, compasses and specialized equipment, there are still plenty of possibilities.

Four signposted nature trails have been established in the Troodos Mountains around Mount Olympus. These are the Artemis, Atalanta, Kalidonia and Persephone trails. In the Akamas Peninsula there are two: the Aphrodite and Adonis. In addition, numerous forest trails have been marked out by the Forestry Department. Further information is available from tourist offices.

MOUNTAIN BIKING

You need a basic level of fitness and cycling skill before trying this seriously, but there are some great mountain-biking areas in Cyprus. If it's real mountains you want, just head for the Troodos Mountains and you will get all the action you can handle.

SKIING

Only in winter, of course! There are two ski lifts and four runs in the Troodos Mountains at Mount Olympus. Skiing is usually – though not always – possible from the beginning of January to the end of March, with ski and boot hire available. **Cyprus Ski Club** ❷ PO Box 22185, 1518 Lefkosia ❶ 22 67 53 40 ❷ Open 09.00–13.00

WATER SPORTS

All resorts have diving schools with trained professional instructors where you can learn the underwater ropes, or go on diving excursions and, if you are more experienced, get close to the colourful marine life that most people see only from a glass-bottomed boat.

◀ *You can learn to dive with trained professional instructors*

LIFESTYLE

Festivals & events

JANUARY
New Year's Day
It is on this day, rather than Christmas Day, that Cypriots exchange seasonal gifts.

FEBRUARY
Carnival
The first day of Lent (50 days before the Orthodox Easter) is known as Green Monday and is the start of the Lenten fast, during which no meat is eaten. In the week before Green Monday, carnivals are held in several towns and villages. The biggest and most colourful is Lemesos's, followed by those of Pafos and Larnaka.

MARCH OR APRIL
Easter
On Easter Saturday, bonfires are lit in the evening, on to which effigies of Judas are thrown. Easter Sunday is celebrated by feasting and the breaking of eggs. Easter is the most important religious event of the year.

MAY
Anthesteria
These flower festivals are held at Pafos, Lemesos and several other towns in May to celebrate spring's return, marked with parades and re-enactments of Greek myths.

JUNE
Lefkosia International Arts Festival
A two-week programme of art exhibitions, theatre, music and dance. It takes place in June at various venues in the city, particularly the Famagusta Gate Cultural Centre.

LIFESTYLE

⬤ *There's no masking the fun at the Lemesos carnival*

Lemesos International Art Festival

For 10 days in June and July, the city's Municipal Gardens is the venue for a programme of music, song and dance by international and local artists.

LIFESTYLE

Kataklysmos
The Festival of the Flood is three days of fairs and water-throwing contests recalling Noah's Ark and the 40 days of the Great Flood.

JULY
Carlsberg Beer Festival
Spreads the message from the Carlsberg brewery, near Lefkosia.

AUGUST
Village Festivals
August and September are popular months for these (check with tourist offices for dates and locations).

SEPTEMBER
Lemesos Wine Festival
At this wildly popular festival, the city's Municipal Gardens are packed with throngs of people filling plastic cups with free wine as fast as the island's many wineries can fill them up. There are also fairground stalls, folk dancing, amusements and food.

DECEMBER
Christmas
The 25th is celebrated in church followed by a family meal at home. Olive twigs and branches, symbols of purity, are placed over doorways and inside houses as decoration, while the Christmas tree symbolizes life and prosperity.

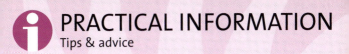

PRACTICAL INFORMATION
Tips & advice

PRACTICAL INFORMATION

Preparing to go

GETTING THERE

The cheapest way to get to Cyprus is to book a package holiday with one of the leading tour operators specializing in Cyprus holidays. You should also check the travel supplements of the weekend newspapers, such as *The Sunday Telegraph* and *The Sunday Times*. They often carry adverts for inexpensive flights, as well as classified adverts for privately owned villas and apartments to rent in most popular holiday destinations.

If your travelling times are flexible, and if you can avoid the school holidays, you can also find some very cheap last-minute deals using the websites for the leading holiday companies.

Further information about Cyprus can be obtained from the **Cyprus Tourism Organisation (CTO)**. Once you reach Cyprus, you will also find CTO offices located all over the island where you can obtain local maps and information. **CTO** ⓐ 17 Hanover Street, London W1S 1YP ⓘ 020 7569 8800 ⓕ 020 7499 4935 ⓦ www.visitcyprus.org.cy

BEFORE YOU LEAVE

Holidays should be about fun and relaxation, so avoid last-minute panics and stress by making your preparations well in advance.

It is not necessary to have inoculations to travel in Europe, but you should make sure you and your family are up to date with the basics, such as tetanus. It is a good idea to pack a small first-aid kit to carry with you, containing plasters, antiseptic cream, travel sickness pills, insect repellent and/or bite relief cream, antihistamine tablets, upset stomach remedies and painkillers. Sun lotion can be more expensive in Cyprus, so it is worth taking a good selection, especially of the higher factor lotions, if you have children with you – and don't forget after-sun cream as well. If you are taking prescription medicines, ensure that you take enough for the duration of your visit – you may find it impossible to obtain the same medicines in Cyprus. It is also worth having a dental check-up before you go.

PRACTICAL INFORMATION

DOCUMENTS

The most important documents you will need are your tickets and your passport. Check well in advance that your passport is up to date and has at least three months left to run (six months is even better). All children, including newborn babies, need their own passport now, unless they are already included on the passport of the person they are travelling with.

It generally takes at least three weeks to process a passport renewal. This can be longer in the run-up to the summer months. For the latest information on how to renew your passport and the processing times, contact the **Passport Agency**. ☎ 0870 521 0410 Ⓦ www.ukpa.gov.uk

You should check the details of your travel tickets well before your departure, ensuring that the timings and dates are correct.

If you are thinking of hiring a car while you are away, you will need to have your UK driving licence with you. If you want more than one driver for the car, the other drivers must have their licence too.

MONEY

You will need some currency before you go, especially if your flight gets you to your destination at the weekend or late in the day after the banks have closed. Traveller's cheques are the safest way to carry money because the money will be refunded if the cheques are lost or stolen. To buy traveller's cheques or exchange money at a bank you may need to give up to a week's notice, depending on the quantity of foreign currency you require.

You can exchange money at the airport before you depart. You should also make sure that your credit, charge and debit cards are up to date – you do not want them to expire mid holiday – and that your credit limit is sufficient to allow you to make those holiday purchases.

Don't forget, too, to check your PIN numbers in case you haven't used them for a while – you may want to draw money from cash dispensers while you are away. Ring your bank or card company and they will help you out.

PRACTICAL INFORMATION

> **EMERGENCY TELEPHONE NUMBERS**
> - Police   112
> - Ambulance   112
> - Fire   112

INSURANCE

Have you got sufficient cover for your holiday? Check that your policy covers you adequately for loss of possessions and valuables, for activities you might want to try – such as scuba-diving, horse-riding, or water sports – and for emergency medical and dental treatment, including flights home if required.

After January 2006, a new EHIC card replaces the E111 form to allow UK visitors access to reduced-cost, and sometimes free state-provided medical treatment in the EEA, which includes EU Cyprus (south). This card is normally valid 3–5 years. For further information, ring EHIC enquiries line: ☏ 0845 605 0707. To apply for a card, ring 0845 606 2030, pick up an application and pre-addressed envelope at the Post Office or visit the Department of Health website ⓦ www.dh.gov.uk and search for 'EHIC card'. It is possible to apply for a card on behalf of your spouse or partner, and for children up to the age of 16, or 19 if they are in full-time education.

CLIMATE

Average summer temperatures range between 21°C to 37°C (70–98°F) in the Central Plain, and from 15°C to 27°C (59–80°F) in the Troodos Mountains. Winters are mild by northern European standards, and temperatures range from 5°C to 17°C (40–60°F) in the Central Plain and from freezing to 9°C (50°F) in the mountains.

PETS

Remember to make arrangements for the care of your pets while you are away – book them into a reputable cat or dog hotel, or make

PRACTICAL INFORMATION

arrangements with a trustworthy neighbour to ensure that they are properly fed, watered and exercised while you are on holiday.

SECURITY

Take sensible precautions to prevent your house being burgled while you are away:

- Cancel milk, newspapers and other regular deliveries so that post and milk does not pile up on the doorstep, indicating that you are away.
- Let the postman know where to leave parcels and bulky mail that will not go through your letterbox – ideally with a next-door neighbour.
- If possible, arrange for a friend or neighbour to visit regularly, closing and opening curtains in the evening and morning, and switching lights on and off to give the impression that the house is being lived in.
- Consider buying electrical timing devices that will switch lights and radios on and off, again to give the impression that there is someone in the house.
- Let Neighbourhood Watch representatives know that you will be away so that they can keep an eye on your home.
- If you have a burglar alarm, make sure that it is serviced and working properly and is switched on when you leave (you may find that your insurance policy requires this). Ensure that a neighbour is able to gain access to the alarm to turn it off if it is set off accidentally.
- If you are leaving cars unattended, put them in a garage, if possible, and leave a key with a neighbour in case the alarm goes off.

AIRPORT PARKING & ACCOMMODATION

If you intend to leave your car in an airport car park while you are away, or stay the night at an airport hotel before or after your flight, you should book well ahead to take advantage of discounts or cheap off-airport parking. Airport accommodation gets booked up several weeks in advance, especially during the height of the holiday season. Check whether the hotel offers free parking for the duration of the holiday – often the savings made on parking costs can significantly reduce the accommodation price.

PRACTICAL INFORMATION

PACKING TIPS

Baggage allowances vary according to the airline, destination and the class of travel, but 20 kg (44 lb) per person is the norm for luggage that is carried in the hold (it usually tells you what the weight limit is on your ticket). You are also allowed one item of cabin baggage weighing no more than 5 kg (11 lb), and measuring 46 by 30 by 23 cm (18 by 12 by 9 inches).

In addition, you can usually carry your duty-free purchases, umbrella, handbag, coat, camera, etc, as hand baggage. Large items – surfboards, golf-clubs, collapsible wheelchairs and pushchairs – are usually charged as extras and it is a good idea to let the airline know in advance that you want to bring these.

CHECK-IN, PASSPORT CONTROL & CUSTOMS

First-time travellers may find the idea of checking in for flights as well as going through passport control and customs – and still making it on to the plane on time – slightly intimidating, but it is all very easy, really.

- Check-in desks usually open two or three hours before the flight is due to depart. Arrive early for the best choice of seats.

- Look for your flight number on the TV monitors in the check-in area, and find the relevant check-in desk. Your tickets will be checked and your luggage taken. Take your boarding card and go to the departure gate. Here your hand luggage will be X-rayed and your passport checked.

- In the departure area, you can shop and relax, but make sure that you continue to check the departure time monitors that tell you when to board – this is usually about 30 minutes before take-off. Go to the departure gate shown on the monitor and follow the instructions given to you by the airline staff.

PRACTICAL INFORMATION

During your stay

AIRPORTS
Cyprus has two international airports: Larnaka is served by charter and scheduled flights, whilst Pafos is mainly a charter airport. Flight information is available 24 hours a day, 7 days a week for Larnaka and Pafos International Airports on ❶ 22 77 88 33. There are numerous charter companies offering flights to Cyprus throughout the year. Scheduled flights from the UK are offered by national carrier **Cyprus Airways** ❸ 5 The Exchange, Brent Cross Gardens, London NW4 3RJ ❶ 0208 359 1333 ❶ 0208 359 1340 ⓦ www.cyprusair.com.cy

BEACHES
In summer, many beaches have lifeguards and a flag safety system. Make sure that you are familiar with the flag system for Cyprus. 'Blue Flag' beaches fulfil the criteria of good quality bathing water, in accordance with the European Union directive, environmental education and information, and beach area management and safety. Other beaches may be safe for swimming but there are unlikely to be lifeguards or life-saving amenities available. Bear in mind that the strong winds that develop in the hotter months can quickly change a safe beach into a not-so-safe one, and some can have strong currents the further out that you go. If in doubt, ask the tourist office, your local representative or at your hotel.

CHILDREN'S ACTIVITIES
Cypriots are very fond of youngsters and there are many playgrounds for children in the tourist areas. Larger hotels often offer child-minding services. Remember to take care of your children when out in the heat and sun, however. Dehydration and sunburn are very real dangers.

CONSULATE
Numbers of all the major consulates on the island can be obtained through directory enquiries on 192. The operators can speak English.

PRACTICAL INFORMATION

CURRENCY
The unit of currency is the Cyprus pound, which is divided into 100 cents. The banking system is modern, and transactions can be negotiated in all leading currencies.

There are no restrictions on the amount of foreign currency imported into Cyprus, although amounts in excess of the equivalent of US$1000 should be declared on arrival to customs – you can then re-export it when you leave. Credit cards are widely accepted wherever tourist facilities are found.

ELECTRICITY
The electricity supply in Cyprus is 220/240V AC. Electric plugs are 3-pin, as in the UK. If you are considering buying electrical appliances to take home, always check that they will work in your country before you buy.

FACILITIES FOR VISITORS WITH DISABILITIES
While the major hotels are designed to allow easy access, visitors with disabilities may experience some frustration elsewhere, especially when trying to negotiate older parts of the towns. Things are slowly changing and facilities are improving, but pavements are often uneven and vary in height. Expect to have to venture onto the road regularly.

GETTING AROUND
Car hire and driving Driving is on the left, and a national or international driving licence is required. Hire cars – those with red number plates and a 'Z' prefix – are widely available, with hire price depending on model and engine capacity. The standard of driving in Cyprus is rather erratic and you should drive with caution.

In case of a breakdown, emergency telephones are located at the side of the major highways. Failing that, the locals are generally happy to help out in whatever way they can.

All of the main towns and villages in Cyprus are well served by petrol stations, but if you are heading further afield it is advisable to fill up beforehand. Petrol stations are open from 06.00 to 19.00 in summer and

PRACTICAL INFORMATION

06.00 to 18.00 in winter on weekdays. They close at 15.00 on Saturdays. On Sundays they are closed all day. In Lefkosia they close at 14.00 on Wednesday, while in the other main towns they are closed on Tuesday afternoons. However, almost all stations have Bank Note Acceptors (BNAs), so in practice you should never run dry.

Public transport The bus service between major towns and tourist areas is fairly good during summer – less so during the winter. There is a standard fare, regardless of how far you travel.

Taxis Within the main towns, these are metered, but tipping is expected. 'Service' taxis operate regularly between the main towns: these are a cheap and easy way to get around. Ask at your hotel for details.

HEALTH MATTERS
Health hazards The heat is the biggest potential danger to your health. Dress in light clothes and try to avoid over-exposure to the sun. Wear a suitable sun lotion and ensure that you consume plenty of liquids (preferably not alcohol) and wear a hat. Remember that the danger of sunburn increases near water.

Pharmacies on the island are operated by highly-qualified staff and are well stocked with prices generally lower than UK. For details of pharmacies on night duty, telephone 192. Details of night pharmacies are also in the *Cyprus Weekly* newspaper.

Emergency treatment is available at local hospitals, but tourists should expect to pay for any treatment they receive. The standard of medical care in Cyprus is high and there are many private clinics offering high-quality and relatively inexpensive treatment. The emergency telephone number is 112 for fire, ambulance or police – all operators speak English (see also page 114).

Water Cyprus's tap water is safe to drink and mostly tastes good. Many people also drink bottled mineral water. Because of several years of drought, water is in short supply and there may be interruptions in supply. Water should not be used wastefully.

PRACTICAL INFORMATION

LANGUAGE

It may seem a difficult language, but the beauty of Greek is that it is phonetic – the spelling of a word often matches its sound. Greeks love to hear visitors attempt to speak it, and it is often worth the extra effort. However, most signs are in Greek and English, and English is so widely – and well – spoken that you can happily trundle through a fortnight without needing a word of Greek.

THE GREEK ALPHABET

Greek	Name	Pronounced
A α	alpha	a
B β	beta	b
Γ γ	gamma	g, but becomes y in front of e and i
Δ δ	delta	d
E ϵ	epsilon	e as in extra
Z ζ	zeta	z
H η	eta	e as in eat
Θ θ	theta	th
I ι	iota	i
K κ	kappa	k
Λ λ	lamda	l
M m	mi	m
N ν	ni	n
Ξ ξ	xi	x
O o	omicron	o
Π π	pi	p
P ρ	rho	r
Σ σ	sigma	s
T τ	taf	t
Y υ	ypsilon	u
Φ φ	phi	ph
X χ	chi	ch as in loch
Ψ ψ	psi	ps
Ω ω	omega	long o

PRACTICAL INFORMATION

General vocabulary

Pronunciation guide	
yes/no	*neh/Okhee*
please/thank you	*parakahLO/efkhareesTO*
hello/goodbye	*YAsoo/andEEo*
good morning/good afternoon/evening	*kahleeMEHRa/kahleeSPEHRa*
good night	*kahleeNEEKHtah*
OK	*enDACKsee*
excuse me/sorry	*signomee*
Help!	*Voylthia!*
today/tomorrow	*siMEHRa/AHvrio*
yesterday	*ektes*

Useful words and phrases

open/closed	*anikTON/klisTON*
right/left	*thexia/aristerA*
How much is it?	*POso kAni?*
Where is a bank/post office?	*Poo Ine i TRApeza?/to tahithromEEo?*
Can we have the bill, please?	*Mas fErnete ton logariasmO, parakalO?*
I don't understand/ Do you speak English?	*Then katalaveno/MilAte AnglikA?*
stamp	*grammatOseemo*
doctor/hospital	*YAHtros/nosokoMEEo*
police	*assteenoMEEa*
I would like...	*Tha Ithela...*
menu	*menOO*
toilets	*tooahLEHtess*
mineral water	*emfialoMENo nerO*
fish/meat	*psarEE/krEas*
beer/wine	*bEEra/krasEE*
Cheers!	*Steen eeyEEa soo!/YAHmas!*
coffee with milk	*kafEs (me gAla)*

PRACTICAL INFORMATION

MEDIA

Three English-language newspapers are published on the island: the daily *Cyprus Mail* (except Mondays), the *Cyprus Weekly* (every Friday) and the *Financial Mirror* (every Wednesday).

Local television programmes are in Greek, although a wide variety of imported programming in English is also screened (with Greek subtitles). There are daily news bulletins in English on both Cyprus television and radio (details in the local press). BFBS (the British Forces Broadcasting Service) also transmits radio programmes in English all over the island.

OPENING HOURS

Shopping and business hours in Cyprus depend on the time of year. Around Greek Orthodox Easter, most places are closed for several days. In the hotter summer months, some premises close for three hours after lunch because of the heat – and because of the Mediterranean custom of having a siesta. Hairdressing salons are closed all day Thursday, but are open all day Saturday.

Shops Summer hours: 08.00–14.00, 17.00–20.00, except Wed 08.00–14.00, Sat 08.00–17.00. These are schedules set by law. Shops can close earlier: for example, this is the case for Lefkosia on Saturdays. However, they cannot open earlier. In winter, they open earlier and close earlier in the afternoon.

Banks Normal banking hours for the public are: summer 08.15–13.00 Monday to Friday and 15.15–16.45 every Monday afternoon. Afternoon facilities for tourists are available at some branches.

PERSONAL COMFORT & SECURITY

Public toilets are found in bus stations and main squares. Marginally cleaner facilities are found in bars, but you should buy a drink if you are using them. Used toilet paper is placed in a waste bin alongside the toilet, not flushed down the loo.

Crime levels are low in Cyprus but you should still take sensible precautions. Lock your car when you have parked and never leave valuables unattended. While the local police are fairly easy-going thanks

PRACTICAL INFORMATION

to the island's low crime rate, reports of theft will be treated seriously. If you should need to report a crime or incident, inform the police immediately and provide them with as many details as possible. Check that they write down the exact information you give them. Make a note yourself of the date you make your statement and the name and direct telephone number of the officer who takes it, as this will be the only reference available for your case.

POST OFFICES

These are open from Monday to Friday, with a limited two-hour service on Saturday mornings. Post offices are closed on Wednesday afternoons, and on other afternoons there is a two-hour service. As opening times fluctuate, it is best to check with your hotel or tour operator. Every letter or card sent from Cyprus requires an extra stamp in addition to the main one – this is a one-cent Refugee Stamp. This stamp raises funds and highlights the cause of the Greek Cypriot refugees created by the Turkish invasion of Cyprus in 1974. Blue folding Aerogrammes are also available but still require the extra Refugee Stamp.

RELIGION

Greek Orthodoxy is the main religion in Cyprus, and Easter is the most important event on the Orthodox calendar. Other denominations hold regular services on the island as well. These are:

Anglican

St Paul's Cathedral, Leoforos Vyronos, Lefkosia   22 67 78 97
St Helena's, Leoforos Gr. Afxentiou, Larnaka   24 65 13 27
Agia Napa Monastery, Agia Napa (English Services)   24 64 28 58
St Barnabas Church, Archiepiskopou Leontiou, Lemesos   25 36 27 13

Roman Catholic

Holy Cross Church, Pyli Pafou, Lefkosia   22 66 21 32
St Catherine's Church, 28 Oktovriou, Lemesos   25 36 29 46
Santa Maria Church, Terra Santa Street, Larnaka   24 64 28 58

PRACTICAL INFORMATION

Others

Saint Maron Maronite Church, Anthoupolis, Lefkosia ☎ 99 68 69 38
Evangelical Church of Cyprus, Larnaka ☎ 24 62 59 27
Armenian Church, Vasili Michailidi, Lefkosia ☎ 24 65 44 35

TELEPHONES

Cyprus Telecommunications Authority (CYTA) public phone boxes are used increasingly rarely these days and unfortunately are often out of order. The majority take phone cards that can be purchased from kiosks and other stores. You can buy pay-as-you-go cards which can be used with most foreign mobile phones for use in Cyprus and abroad. In 2002, Cyprus changed its national telephone numbers from six digits to eight digits. All old six-digit numbers are now preceded by two-digit numbers according to their area, even when calling from within the same district. The main prefixes are: Lefkosia 22, Larnaka 24, Lemesos 25 and Pafos 26.

TIME DIFFERENCES

Local time is two hours ahead of Greenwich Mean Time, except during Cyprus summertime, when it is GMT+3. Cyprus summer time begins on the last Sunday of March and ends on the last Sunday of October.

TIPPING

Not obligatory, but always welcome! The Cyprus Tourism Organisation (CTO) includes a ten per cent service charge on all hotel and restaurant bills. Restaurants are required by law to display their charges.

PHONING ABROAD?

To call an overseas number from Cyprus, dial **oo** (the international access code), then the country code (UK = 44, US = 1), then the area code (minus the inital 0) followed by the number. To call Cyprus from the UK, dial **oo 357** followed by the eight-digit number.

INDEX

INDEX

A

Agia Napa 9, 27-31, 105
Agia Trias 32, 33
Agios Minas 68
Agros 90
airports 23, 115, 117
Akamas Peninsula 9, 10, 11, 62, 64, 105
Akrotiri Peninsula 74-7
Amathous 71-3
Ammochostos (Famagusta) 9, 33
aqueduct 38, 71
Archbishop's palace 15
arts 16, 18, 21, 51, 110, see also icons

B

baths 8, 14, 45, 79
Baths of Aphrodite 10, 105
beaches, see individual resorts
boat trips 29, 31, 42, 44, 53, 62, 77

C

Cape Drepano 59
Cape Greko 28, 34
Cape Kiti 71-3
car hire 118
carnivals 108
castles 8, 10, 44, 51, 75, 105
catacombs 51, 55
cathedral 15
chapels 27, 33, 36, 59
children 9, 28, 39, 58, 105, 117
Choirokoitia neolithic village 10, 71
churches, see individual resorts
climate 8, 114
Coral Bay 58-61
cruises 92-4
currency 113, 118
cycling 29, 34, 76, 86, 107

D

Dheryneia 33
Dinosaur Park 28, 105
diving 28, 107

E

Egypt 92-4
excursions 29, 33, 59, 65-94

F

Fassouri 76
festivals and events 108, 110
Foini 86, 103
food and drink 96-101
forest parks 16, 34
forts 11, 38, 53

G

Galata 84
Geroskipou 52, 103
golf 106
Gourri 68
Greek islands 94
Green Line 10, 14, 19, 21

H

Hala Sultan Tekke 10, 38, 72
handicrafts 12, 22, 41, 46, 54, 90, 102
harbours, see individual resorts
hiking and walking 15, 34, 105, 107

K

Kakopetria 84
karting 28
Keryneia (Kyrenia) 9
Kition 37
Kouklia 12, 80-1
Kourion 11, 78-9

INDEX

L

lace 11, 22, 67, 68, 91, 102
language 120-1
Lara Bay 11
Larnaka 9, 10, 36-41, 108
Larnaka Fort 11, 38
Latsi (Latchi) 9, 62-4
Lefkara 11, 66, 67, 102, 110
Lefkosia (Nicosia) 9, 10, 14-25, 108
Lemesos (Limassol) 9, 10, 42-9, 83, 88, 92, 94, 105, 108, 110

M

markets 22, 41, 46, 54
menu decoder 100-1
monasteries, *see* individual resorts
mosaics 8, 12, 53, 72, 78
mosques, *see* individual resorts
Mount Olympus 9, 11, 85, 107
museums, *see* individual resorts

N

Nicosia, *see* Lefkosia

O

observatory 25
Omodos 12, 90-1
opening hours 122

P

Pafos 9, 12, 50-7, 83, 102, 106, 108
Paralimni 32, 33
Pedoulas 85-6
Pegeia 55, 58-61
Pissouri 42, 77, 80-1
Polis 9, 62-4
post offices 123
Potamos Creek 28, 29

pottery 22, 52, 86, 103
practical information 111-24
Prodromos 85
Protaras 9, 32-5

R

race course 21
red earth 29
Rock of Aphrodite 12, 42, 77, 80-1
ruins, *see* individual resorts

S

salt lakes 10, 72, 76, 105
Sanctuary of Aphrodite 12, 78, 80
Sanctuary of Apollo Ylatis 12, 79
skiing 107
snorkelling 28, 34
Stavrovouni monastery 12, 66, 102
swimming 23, 34

T

telephones 124
tombs 8, 10, 12, 38, 55, 59, 72
Troodos Mountains 8, 9, 11, 12, 82-91
Troodos village 84
Turkish Cyprus 9, 29, 45, 103
turtles 11, 60

V

Varosha 29, 31
Venetian walls 18, 21, 23
visitors with disabilities 118

W

water parks 29, 44
water sports 9, 30, 33, 59, 63, 107
wine 9, 88-91, 98, 110

ACKNOWLEDGEMENTS

ACKNOWLEDGEMENTS

We would like to thank all the photographers, picture libraries and organisations for the loan of the photographs reproduced in this book, to whom copyright in the photograph belongs:
Action Publications (pages 14, 25, 85, 89);
Patricia Aithie (page 25);
JupiterImages Corporation (pages 111, 125);
Pictures Colour Library Ltd (pages 47, 57, 65, 70, 77, 97, 101);
Eric Roberts (pages 20, 63, 69, 95);
Thomas Cook Tour Operations Ltd (pages 1, 5, 11, 13, 31, 32, 39, 49, 53, 58, 61, 65, 79, 81, 87, 93, 99, 103, 104, 106).

We would also like to thank the following for their contribution to this series:
John Woodcock (map and symbols artwork);
Becky Alexander, Patricia Baker, Sophie Bevan, Judith Chamberlain-Webber, Nicky Gyopari, Stephanie Horner, Krystyna Mayer, Robin Pridy (editorial support);
Christine Engert, Suzie Johanson, Richard Lloyd, Richard Peters, Alistair Plumb, Jane Prior, Barbara Theisen, Ginny Zeal, Barbara Zuñiga (design support).

Send your thoughts to
books@thomascook.com

- **Found a beach bar, peaceful stretch of sand or must-see sight that we don't feature?**
- **Like to tip us off about any information that needs a little updating?**
- **Want to tell us what you love about this handy, little guidebook and more importantly how we can make it even handier?**

Then here's your chance to tell all! Send us ideas, discoveries and recommendations today and then look out for your valuable input in the next edition of this title. And, as an extra 'thank you' from Thomas Cook Publishing, you'll be automatically entered into our exciting monthly prize draw.

Email to the above address or write to:
HotSpots Project Editor, Thomas Cook Publishing, PO Box 227, Unit 15/16, Coningsby Road, Peterborough PE3 8SB, UK.